The Essential Quiz Collection

This is a Parragon book
This edition published in 2004

Parragon
Queen Street House
4 Queen Street
Bath BA1 1HE, UK

This edition © Parragon 2003
Illustrations courtesy of Slatter-Anderson, London
Cover courtesy of Kit Rocket

This Book was created by Magpie Books,
an imprint of Constable & Robinson Ltd

ISBN 1-40544-286-7

Printed in China

A copy of the British Library Cataloguing-in-Publication
Date is available from the British Library

The Essential
Quiz Collection

p

Quiz 1

Answers on page 4

1. What does Volkswagen mean?

2. What part did Matthew Simmonds play in the history of Manchester United?

3. Into which sea does the River Jordan flow?

4. Which golfer completed the Grand Slam of the amateur and professional Opens of both the USA and Britain in 1930?

5. Which singer was 'Moonlighting' in 1975?

6. What is the zodiac symbol for Gemini?

7. Which town on the south coast of England became a city as part of the Millennium celebrations?

8. Which newsreader presented the first series of *The People Versus*?

9. Which Scottish rugby player married a TV sports presenter in 2001?

10. What is a garganey?

11. Which boxer was banned for taking a bite out of Evander Holyfield's ear in 1997?

12. In which English county would you find St Michael's Mount?

13. Whose wife was turned into a pillar of salt?

14. Which novelist is credited with the introduction of pillar boxes?

15. Who directed the film *Blow-Up*?

16. What was the maiden name of Jane Austen's heroine *Emma*?

Answers to page 4
QUIZ 3: **1.** Brian Lara **2.** Time And Relative Dimension In Space **3.** Dead Sea **4.** David Lean **5.** Dartmoor **6.** George IV **7.** *High Road* **8.** Holland **9.** Lennox Lewis and Frank Bruno **10.** Kent **11.** *Peyton Place* **12.** Robert Carlyle **13.** Carina **14.** Kneecap **15.** Terry Gilliam **16.** Adrian Moorhouse

Quiz 2

Answers on page 5

1. Who is the brains behind the band Gorillaz?

2. What is a pangolin also known as?

3. From which country does the lambada dance originate?

4. Where is the Kuril Trench?

5. The Murray-Darling is the longest river in which country?

6. Which building is the principal residence of the Archbishop of Canterbury?

7. Which golfer lost a six-shot lead in the final round of the 1996 US Masters?

8. What size paper is half of an A4 sheet?

9. Who was Luke Skywalker's father?

10. What is a jansky a unit of?

11. Brian Bennett was the drummer with which instrumental group?

12. Who owned a dog called Cracker in *Brookside*?

13. Which American ice skater was accused of plotting to break her rival's legs?

14. Who would have been called the Biblical 'Orpah' had the midwife not spelt the name wrongly on the birth certificate?

15. Which South American country was named after an Italian city?

16. Who wrote *Treasure Island* and *Kidnapped*?

Answers to page 5
QUIZ 4: **1.** Bram Stoker **2.** France **3.** Mick Taylor **4.** Colombia and Peru **5.** Neville Chamberlain
6. Richard Harris **7.** Kevin **8.** Toothpaste **9.** Quick-drying ink **10.** Natalie Imbruglia **11.** Weymouth
12. Eddie Edwards **13.** *Shooting Stars* **14.** Minnehaha **15.** 10ft **16.** Beau and Jeff

Quiz 3

Answers on page 2

1. Which cricketer broke the world record for the highest individual Test score with 375 for West Indies against England in 1994?

2. What does TARDIS stand for?

3. Which sea is nearly 1,300ft below sea level?

4. Who won an Oscar for his direction of *Lawrence of Arabia*?

5. In which national park is Yes Tor?

6. With which King of England did Caroline of Brunswick endure a loveless marriage?

7. Which TV soap is set in Glendarroch?

8. What nationality were Teach-In, winners of the 1975 Eurovision Song Contest?

9. In 1993, which two men took part in the first 20th-century World Heavyweight Championship fight between two British boxers?

10. The Isle of Sheppey is part of which English county?

11. Which Grace Metalious novel became a successful TV series starring Mia Farrow and Ryan O'Neal?

12. Who played TV detective Hamish Macbeth?

13. Which constellation is represented as a ship's keel?

14. What part of the human body is the patella?

15. Which American animator was a member of the *Monty Python* team?

16. Which English swimmer won the 100 metres breaststroke at the 1988 Seoul Olympics?

Answers to page 2
QUIZ 1: **1.** 'People's car' **2.** He was the Crystal Palace fan at whom Eric Cantona launched his infamous flying kick in 1995 **3.** The Dead Sea **4.** Bobby Jones **5.** Leo Sayer **6.** Twins **7.** Brighton **8.** Kirsty Young **9.** Kenny Logan **10.** A teal-like bird **11.** Mike Tyson **12.** Cornwall **13.** Lot **14.** Anthony Trollope **15.** Michelangelo Antonioni **16.** Woodhouse

Quiz 4

Answers on page 3

1. Who created Dracula?

2. In 1778, which country introduced the first state-controlled brothels?

3. Who was the first replacement for Brian Jones in The Rolling Stones?

4. Which two South American countries have borders with Ecuador?

5. Which British Prime Minister returned from Munich in 1938 clutching a piece of paper and a promise of 'peace in our time'?

6. Which Irish actor played Oliver Cromwell in the 1970 film?

7. Which boy's name means 'handsome at birth'?

8. A Roman mixture of vinegar, honey and salt was the first known example of what?

9. For what was Quink an abbreviation?

10. Which former *Neighbours* actress was 'Torn' in 1997?

11. Portland Bill is connected by road to which resort?

12. Which British ski jumper was ironically nicknamed 'The Eagle'?

13. Which TV series featured the Dove from Above?

14. Who was married to Hiawatha?

15. How high is a basketball hoop from the floor?

16. Who are the actor sons of Lloyd Bridges?

Answers to page 3
QUIZ 2: **1.** Damon Albarn **2.** Scaly anteater **3.** Brazil **4.** In the Pacific Ocean **5.** Australia **6.** Lambeth Palace **7.** Greg Norman **8.** A5 **9.** Darth Vader **10.** Radiation **11.** The Shadows **12.** Jimmy Corkhill **13.** Tonya Harding **14.** Oprah Winfrey **15.** Venezuela (Venice) **16.** Robert Louis Stevenson

Quiz 5

Answers on page 8

1. On which TV show did music-hall comedian Arthur Atkinson appear?

2. Which nun won the Nobel Peace Prize in 1979?

3. Which former boxer made a citizen's arrest at Gatwick Airport in August 2001?

4. Which dog is sometimes called a bobtail?

5. Which French composer is best known for his 'Symphonie Espagnole'?

6. Which space-age hero was created by Kenny Everett?

7. Aboard which ship did Captain Scott sail to the Antarctic in 1901?

8. Who was Othello's wife?

9. How many sides are there to an octagon?

10. What was the title of All Saints' first UK number one single?

11. Gibraltar Point is situated to the south of which east-coast resort?

12. At which sport do Neil Hodgson and John Reynolds compete?

13. Which explorer introduced the potato and tobacco to Europe?

14. What does a phonophobe fear?

15. Who was Britain's first Christian martyr?

16. The resort of Biarritz is on which coast of France?

Answers to page 8

QUIZ 7: **1.** Trevor Brooking **2.** George Harrison **3.** Jimmy 'Schnozzle' Durante **4.** Marcel Marceau **5.** Geri Halliwell **6.** Ankara **7.** A half **8.** William of Orange **9.** Wilmington **10.** *David Copperfield* **11.** On the moon **12.** The March Hare **13.** Jamaica **14.** Pauline **15.** Prince **16.** Gloucestershire

Quiz 6

Answers on page 9

1. Which lead singer with university band The Ugly Rumours has gone on to achieve fame in a different field?

2. Which cartoon lion's catchphrase was 'Heavens to Murgatroyd'?

3. What is the term for an over in cricket where no runs are scored?

4. What bodily function can exceed a speed of 200mph?

5. In which country's currency do 100 centavos make a sucre?

6. For which film did Kevin Spacey win an Oscar for Best Actor in 1999?

7. Who wrote *Tess of the D'Urbervilles*?

8. Immortalised by the rhyme, the bridge of Avignon in France crosses which river?

9. Mn is the chemical symbol for which element?

10. As whom is Princess Aurora better known?

11. What is Spencer Perceval's unfortunate claim to fame?

12. Which band frequently supported Bob Dylan?

13. In which English city would you find The Shambles?

14. How long did the Hundred Years War last?

15. Which German composer, whose name was adopted by a 20th-century singer, wrote the fairy opera *Hansel and Gretel*?

16. Which house on the Isle of Wight was one of Queen Victoria's homes?

Answers to page 9
QUIZ 8: **1.** A sperm whale **2.** Mansfield Town **3.** Colon **4.** The Pharos **5.** Austria and Prussia **6.** Nazareth **7.** Austria and Italy **8.** Brighton **9.** Featherweight **10.** Mark Williams **11.** Cancer **12.** Tinkerbell **13.** Prune **14.** Robert Mitchum **15.** Billie Jean King **16.** Hercule Poirot

Quiz 7

Answers on page 6

1. Of which footballer did Brian Clough remark: 'Floats like a butterfly, and stings like one'?

2. Who played guitar under the name of L'Angelo Mysterioso on Cream's 'Badge'?

3. Which vaudeville comedian had his bulbous nose insured for $100,000?

4. Who spoke the only word in Mel Brooks' *Silent Movie*?

5. Which singer pleaded 'Look At Me' in 1999?

6. What is the capital of Turkey?

7. What is the square root of a quarter?

8. Which Dutchman became King of England in 1688?

9. Which port in Delaware was formerly known as Fort Christina?

10. Betsey Trotwood is a character in which Dickens novel?

11. Where is the Marsh of Decay?

12. Who put butter in the Mad Hatter's watch?

13. The film *Cool Runnings* was based on the true story of which country's bobsled team at the 1998 Winter Olympics?

14. What is the name of Adrian Mole's mother?

15. Who wrote Sinead O'Connor's hit 'Nothing Compares 2 U'?

16. Which county won all three one-day cricket titles in 2000?

Answers to page 6
QUIZ 5: **1.** *The Fast Show* **2.** Mother Teresa **3.** Nigel Benn **4.** Old English sheepdog **5.** Edouard Lalo **6.** Captain Kremmen **7.** The *Discovery* **8.** Desdemona **9.** Eight **10.** 'Never Ever' **11.** Skegness **12.** Motorcycle racing **13.** Sir Walter Raleigh **14.** Noise **15.** St Alban **16.** West

Quiz 8

Answers on page 7

1. What is a cachalot?

2. Which Football League team plays at Field Mill?

3. What can be part of the large intestine or a punctuation mark?

4. Which lighthouse was one of the Seven Wonders of the World?

5. Which two countries fought the Seven Weeks' War in 1866?

6. Dan McCafferty was lead singer with which seventies band?

7. The Brenner Pass links which two countries?

8. In which English seaside resort are The Lanes?

9. In boxing which is heavier – featherweight or flyweight?

10. Which Welsh snooker player is the namesake of a member of *The Fast Show* team?

11. Which zodiac sign has the symbol of a crab?

12. What was the name of the fairy in *Peter Pan*?

13. What is a dried plum called?

14. Which Hollywood actor served 59 days in a California jail in 1948 for possessing narcotics?

15. Which tennis ace was the subject of Elton John's 'Philadelphia Freedom'?

16. Which literary detective makes great use of his 'little grey cells'?

Answers to page 7
QUIZ 6: **1.** Tony Blair **2.** Snagglepuss **3.** Maiden **4.** A sneeze **5.** Ecuador **6.** *American Beauty* **7.** Thomas Hardy **8.** Rhone **9.** Manganese **10.** Sleeping Beauty **11.** He is the only British Prime Minister to have been assassinated **12.** The Band **13.** York **14.** 116 years **15.** Engelbert Humperdinck **16.** Osborne House

Quiz 9

Answers on page 12

1. Who laid out his BBC boss with a turkey?

2. What has 336 dimples?

3. What is a cupel used for?

4. Whose 2001 album was titled *Fever*?

5. Jennifer Ehle is the daughter of which actress?

6. On which river does Newbury stand?

7. Which band's first hit was 'Pictures of Matchstick Men'?

8. How many players are there on a basketball team?

9. Who was the original choice to play Frank Spencer?

10. Who was Britain's only Conservative Prime Minister between 1964 and 1979?

11. In which country is Odense?

12. Who was always coming up with 'cunning plans'?

13. Which actor's real name was Walter Matuschanskavasky?

14. Which African country was ruled by Idi Amin in the 1970s?

15. Which jockey beat cancer to win the 1981 Grand National on Aldaniti?

16. One of which composer's notebooks fetched £2.3 million in auction at Sotheby's in May 1987?

Answers to page 12
QUIZ 11: **1.** Macy Gray **2.** Johnny Vaughan **3.** Talking Heads **4.** Russia **5.** Wrestling **6.** New Zealand **7.** A large antelope **8.** Ice skating **9.** Botany Bay **10.** Hellas **11.** Kenny Everett **12.** Medici **13.** Golf **14.** Pickettywitch **15.** Sheffield **16.** Topper

Quiz 10

Answers on page 13

1. What job did Ricky Tomlinson's Mike Bassett hold in a 2001 film?

2. What is the name for a female calf?

3. Which mallet-wielding TV presenter gave Chris Evans his big break?

4. In which year did Creedence Clearwater Revival have a UK number one hit with 'Bad Moon Rising'?

5. Bismarck is the capital of which American state?

6. What did former Manchester United goalkeeper Alex Stepney once do while shouting at a team-mate?

7. Keanu Reeves, Dennis Hopper and Sandra Bullock starred in which 1994 thriller movie?

8. Whereabouts in the human body is the lacrimal gland?

9. Helen Burns is a character in which Charlotte Brontë novel?

10. Which country marks the western border of Oman?

11. The Needles can be found on which island?

12. Who composed the opera *The Rake's Progress*?

13. Norman Greenbaum and Doctor and the Medics had UK number one hits at 16-year intervals with which song?

14. Which town in North Yorkshire is famous for its annual bed race?

15. Which artificial stimulant was banned from the World Worm-Charming Championships?

16. The treacherous Goodwin Sands are situated off the coast of which English county?

Answers to page 13
QUIZ 12: **1.** Lucy Liu **2.** Truth **3.** Woodlouse **4.** Diving **5.** Elephant **6.** Accrington, Barrow, Gateshead and Bradford Park Avenue **7.** John Laurie (Frazer) **8.** Sirius (Dog Star) **9.** The Vatican **10.** Ten **11.** Tenerife **12.** Honeybus **13.** Tennessee **14.** Yellow **15.** The Iron Age **16.** Morocco

Quiz 11

Answers on page 10

1. Which singer did Lord Snowdon call the rudest woman he'd ever photographed?

2. Which former *Big Breakfast* presenter was in something *'Orrible* in 2001?

3. Which US band on the road to nowhere were originally called The Artistics?

4. With what country was Berwick-upon-Tweed officially at war for 110 years until 1966?

5. At which sport could you fall victim to a flying mare or a half Nelson?

6. The Chatham Islands belong to which country?

7. What is a kudu?

8. Canada's Kurt Browning was a world champion at which sport?

9. Whereabouts in Australia did Captain Cook land in 1770?

10. What is the Greek name for Greece?

11. Whose TV characters included Mr Angry of Mayfair and Marcel Wave?

12. Which family ruled Florence from 1434 to 1737?

13. Of what sport is Sergio Garcia a leading exponent?

14. Which group had 'That Same Old Feeling' in 1970?

15. In which city is the Crucible Theatre, venue for the World Snooker Championships?

16. What was the name of Hopalong Cassidy's horse?

Answers to page 10
QUIZ 9: **1.** Alan Partridge **2.** A golf ball **3.** Assaying gold **4.** Kylie Minogue **5.** Rosemary Harris **6.** River Kennet **7.** Status Quo **8.** Five **9.** Norman Wisdom **10.** Edward Heath **11.** Denmark **12.** Baldrick **13.** Walter Matthau **14.** Uganda **15.** Bob Champion **16.** Mozart

Quiz 12

Answers on page 11

1. Who plays Ling in *Ally McBeal* and Alex in *Charlie's Angels: The Movie*?

2. What does the name of the Russian newspaper *Pravda* mean?

3. Which common garden creature is really a crustacean?

4. At what sport does Greg Louganis participate?

5. What animal has a gestation period of 21 months?

6. Which four former Football League clubs played in the Unibond League Premier Division in 2001–2?

7. Which member of the *Dad's Army* cast was actually in the Home Guard during the Second World War?

8. Which is the brightest star in the sky?

9. Where is the Sistine Chapel?

10. How many frames are there in a game of tenpin bowling?

11. Which is the largest of the Canary Islands?

12. Which band couldn't let Maggie go in 1968?

13. Nashville is the capital of which American state?

14. What colour are the flowers of a tansy?

15. What age followed the Bronze Age?

16. In which country is the port of Tangier?

Answers to page 11
QUIZ 10: **1.** England football manager **2.** Heifer **3.** Timmy Mallett **4.** 1969 **5.** North Dakota
6. Dislocated his jaw **7.** *Speed* **8.** The eye **9.** *Jane Eyre* **10.** Yemen **11.** Isle of Wight **12.** Stravinsky
13. 'Spirit In The Sky' **14.** Knaresborough **15.** Washing-up liquid **16.** Kent

Quiz 13

Answers on page 16

1. What is Muckle Flugga's geographical significance?

2. Who was the winged horse in Greek mythology?

3. Which 20th-century playwright penned *Equus* and *Amadeus*?

4. How many England caps did goalkeeper Peter Shilton win?

5. Which American jockey was nicknamed 'The Shoe'?

6. Which US record producer created the 'wall of sound'?

7. Who longed to become a Yellowcoat in *Hi-De-Hi!*?

8. In which country is Spitsbergen?

9. Which American paediatrician wrote *The Common Sense Book of Baby and Child Care*?

10. Which singer wanted to 'Fly Away' in 1999?

11. In which century did the Chinese Ming dynasty start?

12. Who was Pope during the Second World War?

13. What is the state capital of New Jersey?

14. What takes place at Cadwell Park and Mallory Park?

15. Which actor played Daredevil in the 2003 film?

16. Which two acts topped the UK singles charts with 'Mary's Boy Child'?

Answers to page 16
QUIZ 15: **1.** Shoulder-blade **2.** The Bangles **3.** *Sense and Sensibility* **4.** Mr Venables **5.** Indiana
6. Kalahari **7.** Queens Park Rangers **8.** Kabul **9.** Harold Wilson **10.** Austrian **11.** Greece and Turkey
12. 180 **13.** North America **14.** The Boswells **15.** Blondie **16.** Jose Maria Olazabal

Quiz 14

Answers on page 17

1. Which King of England employed a groom whose job it was to wipe the royal bottom?

2. Which former England rugby captain famously split up with Gary Lineker's sister-in-law?

3. Which actress won an Oscar at the age of 80 in 1989 for *Driving Miss Daisy*?

4. Who hosts *They Think It's All Over*?

5. In which county is Chepstow?

6. How many square yards are there in an acre?

7. What is the fifth book of the New Testament?

8. Which singer's real name is Richard Melville Hall?

9. Who played Jim Rockford in *The Rockford Files*?

10. Septicaemia is the technical term for what?

11. Who won the Formula One World Drivers' Championship in 1988, 1990 and 1991?

12. What is the minimum number of games needed to win a set of tennis?

13. In which London park is the Serpentine?

14. Which is the only Australian state to have borders with five others?

15. The name of which English county is sometimes abbreviated to Salop?

16. What is a sidewinder?

Answers to page 17
QUIZ 16: **1.** Stevie Wonder **2.** *Braveheart* **3.** Tessa Sanderson **4.** *Fawlty Towers* **5.** Benjamin Disraeli **6.** Jane Fonda **7.** 12 **8.** Jethro Tull **9.** Leicester City **10.** Northumberland **11.** Coral Sea **12.** Mussorgsky **13.** All are born-again Christians **14.** 'When Smokey Sings' **15.** Cob **16.** Greg Medavoy

Quiz 15

Answers on page 14

1. What part of the human body is the scapula?

2. Which girl band, who split up shortly after a 1989 number one, reformed in 2001?

3. Elinor Dashwood was a heroine in which Jane Austen novel?

4. What was the name of the prison governor in *Porridge*?

5. Fort Wayne and Gary are towns in which American state?

6. The Okavango is the only permanent river in which southern African desert?

7. Which club staged the first Football League game on artificial turf?

8. What is the capital of Afghanistan?

9. Which political rival called former British Prime Minister Edward Heath 'a shiver looking for a spine to run up'?

10. What nationality is ex-Formula One World Champion Niki Lauda?

11. Which two countries signed the Treaty of Lausanne in 1923?

12. How many degrees do the hands of a clock pass through to travel from three o'clock to nine o'clock?

13. In which continent is the Okefenokee swamp?

14. What was the name of the family in *Bread*?

15. Who are the only American group to have had UK number one hits in the seventies, eighties and nineties?

16. Which Spanish golfer's nickname is 'Olly'?

Answers to page 14
QUIZ 13: **1.** It is the most northerly island in the British Isles **2.** Pegasus **3.** Peter Shaffer **4.** 125 **5.** Willie Shoemaker **6.** Phil Spector **7.** Peggy **8.** Norway **9.** Dr Spock **10.** Lenny Kravitz **11.** 14th **12.** Pius XII **13.** Trenton **14.** Motor-cycle racing **15.** Ben Affleck **16.** Harry Belafonte and Boney M

Quiz 16

Answers on page 15

1. Who played harmonica on Chaka Khan's 'I Feel For You'?

2. Which Mel Gibson movie won the 1995 Academy Award for Best Picture?

3. Who was the first British athlete to win an Olympic gold medal in a throwing event?

4. Miss Tibbs and Miss Gatsby were resident guests at which establishment?

5. Which 19th-century British Prime Minister became the Earl of Beaconsfield?

6. Which member of a famous acting family starred in *Cat Ballou* and *Barbarella*?

7. In poetic terms, how many syllables are there in an Alexandrine?

8. With which band did Ian Anderson play the flute and sing?

9. From which club did Liverpool sign footballer Emile Heskey?

10. In which English county is Alnwick?

11. Which is the biggest sea in the world?

12. Who composed 'Pictures From an Exhibition'?

13. What do Cannon and Ball, Samantha Fox and Glenn Hoddle have in common?

14. What was the title of ABC's tribute to Smokey Robinson?

15. What can be a male swan or a bread roll?

16. Who does Gordon Clapp play in *NYPD Blue*?

Answers to page 15
QUIZ 14: **1.** Henry VIII **2.** Will Carling **3.** Jessica Tandy **4.** Nick Hancock **5.** Gwent **6.** 4,840
7. The Acts **8.** Moby **9.** James Garner **10.** Blood poisoning **11.** Ayrton Senna **12.** Six **13.** Hyde Park
14. South Australia **15.** Shropshire **16.** A rattlesnake

Quiz 17

Answers on page 20

1. What was wrong with the film title *Krakatoa, East of Java*?

2. Which golfer's chances of winning the 2001 British Open vanished when he was penalised for carrying too many clubs in his bag?

3. Dublin is the capital of which Irish province?

4. Which French town has a reputation for miraculous cures?

5. Eternal's 1996 hit 'Someday' was taken from which film?

6. Which footballer was the first person to refuse to be the subject of *This Is Your Life*?

7. What breed of dog is a clumber?

8. Who contributed guest vocals on UB40's version of 'I Got You Babe'?

9. If you ordered 'moules' in a French restaurant, what would you expect to be served?

10. According to Scottish superstition, which two colours should never be worn together?

11. Which crime has a potential 324 different combinations?

12. The name of which Indonesian city means 'place of victory'?

13. According to Alaskan state law, what is it illegal to look at from the window of an aircraft?

14. Which European city staged the 1928 Olympics?

15. What is the common name for the plant *Impatiens*?

16. Who rowed through a storm with her father one night in 1838 to save nine shipwrecked souls off the Farne Islands?

Answers to page 20
QUIZ 19: **1.** Lake Victoria **2.** Hippopotamus **3.** Sn **4.** William Congreve **5.** Four **6.** Jerry Lewis **7.** Real Madrid **8.** Mini cab driver **9.** Craig Douglas **10.** Sir Geoffrey Howe **11.** 'Turnip' **12.** Trent **13.** Isosceles triangle **14.** A cold soup **15.** Isle of Man **16.** *Uncle Remus*

Quiz 18

Answers on page 21

1. In music, what is meant by the term 'legato'?

2. Why is a cheetah unlike other cats?

3. What is pumpernickel?

4. In 1983, what became the first a cappella song to top the UK singles chart?

5. Which South African golfer won the US Open twice in the 1990s?

6. Who was the Roman god of fire?

7. Which Spaniard conquered the Aztec empire in the 16th century?

8. What kind of hopefuls attend RADA?

9. In which continent is the River Plate?

10. In motor-racing, who was the first winner of the World Drivers' Championship?

11. The thylacine is another name for which carnivorous marsupial?

12. Who took 'Ma Baker' to number two in the charts in 1977?

13. What is the national emblem of Canada?

14. Who was known as 'The Girl With The Million Dollar Legs'?

15. Ed Koch, the Mayor of New York in 1984, played himself in which Muppet movie?

16. About which London street did Gerry Rafferty sing in 1978?

Answers to page 21
QUIZ 20: **1.** Jean-Claude Van Damme **2.** Durex **3.** The telephone answering machine **4.** *Ben-Hur*
5. Rawlplug **6.** Reita Faria **7.** Pauline Collins **8.** Norway **9.** Texas **10.** Fishing (for eels) **11.** God of marriage **12.** Australia **13.** *Danger Man* **14.** Robert Dudley **15.** Left **16.** Jack Lemmon

Quiz 19

Answers on page 18

1. Which lake is the source of the White Nile?

2. Which animal has been responsible for more human deaths than any other?

3. What is the chemical symbol for tin?

4. Which playwright penned *The Way of the World* in 1700?

5. How many sides does a trapezium have?

6. Who starred in the original version of *The Nutty Professor*?

7. Which Spanish football team won the European Champions' League in 1998 and 2000?

8. What did *Coronation Street*'s Don Brennan do for a living?

9. Which former milkman had a number one hit with 'Only Sixteen'?

10. Of which fellow politician did Denis Healey say: 'Being attacked in the House by him is like being savaged by a dead sheep'?

11. What was the nickname of agricultural reformer Charles Townshend?

12. Which river – the third longest in England – rises in the South Pennines and flows through the Midlands to the Humber?

13. What is the name for a triangle where two sides and two angles are the same?

14. What is gazpacho?

15. Whose parliament is called the Tynwald?

16. Brer Rabbit was a character in which series of talk tales by Joel Chandler Harris?

Answers to page 18
QUIZ 17: **1.** Krakatoa is west of Java **2.** Ian Woosnam **3.** Leinster **4.** Lourdes **5.** *The Hunchback of Notre Dame* **6.** Danny Blanchflower **7.** Spaniel **8.** Chrissie Hynde **9.** Mussels **10.** Red and green **11.** The murder in Cluedo **12.** Jakarta **13.** A moose **14.** Amsterdam **15.** Bizzy Lizzy **16.** Grace Darling

Quiz 20

Answers on page 19

1. Who is known as 'The Muscles From Brussels'?

2. Which product takes its name from its three prime requisites – durability, reliability and excellence?

3. The Electronic Secretary was the prototype of which device?

4. For which movie did Charlton Heston win a Best Actor Oscar in 1959?

5. London building contractor John J. Rawlings was responsible for which 20th-century invention?

6. Which Miss India won the Miss World contest in 1966?

7. Which actress left *The Liver Birds* after just five episodes?

8. Which Scandinavian country extends the farthest north?

9. Whose 1999 album was titled *The Hush*?

10. What are you doing if you are sniggling?

11. Which god was Hymen in Greek mythology?

12. Which country won the 1999 Cricket World Cup?

13. Who was John Drake otherwise known as on TV?

14. What was the name of the Earl of Leicester who was a prominent member of the court of Elizabeth I?

15. Anything 'sinister' refers to which side?

16. Which Hollywood actor was born John Uhler III?

Answers to page 19
QUIZ 18: **1.** Smoothly **2.** It can't retract its claws **3.** A type of bread **4.** 'Only You' by The Flying Pickets **5.** Ernie Els **6.** Vulcan **7.** Hernán Cortés **8.** Actors **9.** South America **10.** Dr Giuseppe Farina **11.** Tasmanian wolf **12.** Boney M **13.** Maple leaf **14.** Betty Grable **15.** *The Muppets Take Manhattan* **16.** 'Baker Street'

Quiz 21

Answers on page 24

1. What Beverly Hills number was the title of a TV series?

2. Which Tomb Raider won an Oscar for Best Supporting Actress in the film *Girl, Interrupted*?

3. Which motor-racing circuit has a corner called Bus Stop?

4. Which country was controlled by the fascist Iron Guard in the 1930s?

5. What is hyperbole?

6. In military terms, what is the opposite of a hawk?

7. What was Louis Balfour's favourite type of music in *The Fast Show*?

8. Where in Britain would you find Lewis with Harris?

9. What is the next prime number after 37?

10. In which country is the Snake river?

11. Which city in the world has the largest population?

12. Where was the Store Baet suspension bridge opened in 1997?

13. What is Australia's equivalent of the County Cricket Championship?

14. What animals are affected by scrapie?

15. Who was elected President of the NUM in 1981?

16. Joshua Reynolds was an English painter in which century?

Answers to page 24
QUIZ 23: **1.** Donnie Wahlberg **2.** Eddystone **3.** Spain and USA **4.** Shrews **5.** English parliament
6. Kate Winslet **7.** European bison **8.** Brazilian **9.** Abominable Snowman **10.** Boa **11.** Mr Micawber
12. Margaret Drabble **13.** A fish **14.** Cursor **15.** Croydon **16.** Claire King

Quiz 22

Answers on page 25

1. Who won the first of his five Olympic gold medals in the coxed fours in 1984?

2. What was the first name of the French novelist Proust?

3. Which Pound was a US poet?

4. Which Irish athlete won a gold at 5,000 and 10,000 metres at the 1998 European Championships?

5. Which English artist exhibited a shark preserved in a tank of formaldehyde?

6. In which year did Abba have a worldwide hit with 'Dancing Queen'?

7. Who wrote *The Madness of King George*?

8. Which residential district of west London was laid out in squares by Thomas Cubitt?

9. In which country is Arnhem Land?

10. In which city is the Ashton Gate football ground?

11. On which river is the Kariba Dam?

12. Which band released the album *Jollification*?

13. Which Formula One team was founded in 1966 by a New Zealand driver?

14. Oakland is linked by bridge to which Californian city?

15. Which journalist was editor of *Punch* from 1953 to 1957?

16. What is the name of the loading mark painted on the hull of merchant ships?

Answers to page 25
QUIZ 24: **1.** CAT scan **2.** Camp David **3.** Matt Biondi **4.** Ramadan **5.** Oysters **6.** Congress of Vienna **7.** U2 **8.** Chile and Argentina **9.** Swindon **10.** Red squirrel **11.** Ure **12.** Star Wars **13.** Russell Crowe **14.** Personal identification number **15.** Lake **16.** Cello

Quiz 23

Answers on page 22

1. Which member of the New Kids on the Block appeared in the 1999 movie *The Sixth Sense*?

2. Which lighthouse is situated 14 miles south of Plymouth?

3. Which two countries have mountain ranges called Sierra Nevada?

4. What can be pygmy, elephant or hero?

5. What was the Rump in the 17th century?

6. Which English film star made her debut in *Heavenly Creatures*?

7. A wisent is another name for which animal?

8. What nationality was racing driver Nelson Piquet?

9. What was supposedly first spotted in the Himalayas in 1832?

10. The anaconda is a species of which snake?

11. Which *David Copperfield* character is thought to be based on Dickens' own father?

12. Who wrote *The Millstone* and *The Gates of Ivory*?

13. What is a dory?

14. What symbol indicates the current entry position on a computer screen?

15. Fairfield Halls are in which London borough?

16. Which former *Emmerdale* actress starred in *Bad Girls*?

Answers to page 22
QUIZ 21: **1.** 90210 **2.** Angelina Jolie **3.** Spa **4.** Romania **5.** Exaggeration **6.** Dove **7.** Jazz **8.** Outer Hebrides **9.** 41 **10.** USA **11.** Tokyo **12.** Denmark **13.** Sheffield Shield **14.** Sheep and goats **15.** Arthur Scargill **16.** 18th

Quiz 24

Answers on page 23

1. What is a computerised axial tomography scan better known as?

2. What is the official country home of US Presidents?

3. Which American swimmer won eight Olympic gold medals between 1984 and 1992?

4. What is the name given to the month of Muslim fasting?

5. With which sea food is Whitstable associated?

6. Which Congress agreed the settlement of Europe after the Napoleonic Wars?

7. Which band released the 1991 album *Achtung Baby*?

8. Which two countries own regions of Tierra del Fuego?

9. Diana Dors and Melinda Messenger both hailed from which town?

10. Which native British rodent has the Latin name *Sciurus*?

11. On which river does Ripon stand?

12. What was the popular name for Ronald Reagan's Strategic Defense Initiative?

13. Which actor played a former tobacco company executive who blew the whistle on the industry in the 1999 movie *The Insider*?

14. What does PIN stand for?

15. What kind of geographical feature is an oxbow?

16. What musical instrument does Julian Lloyd Webber play?

Answers to page 23
QUIZ 22: **1.** Steve Redgrave **2.** Marcel **3.** Ezra Pound **4.** Sonia O'Sullivan **5.** Damien Hirst **6.** 1976 **7.** Alan Bennett **8.** Belgravia **9.** Australia **10.** Bristol **11.** Zambezi **12.** Lightning Seeds **13.** McLaren **14.** San Francisco **15.** Malcolm Muggeridge **16.** Plimsoll line

Quiz 25

Answers on page 28

1. How many property squares are there on a Monopoly board?

2. Which singer/actress has been married to Jim Kerr and Liam Gallagher?

3. Which English actress played one of Ross's wives in *Friends*?

4. Which 17-year-old American became the youngest winner of a Grand Slam tennis title when he captured the 1989 French Open?

5. What is the name for a ring-shaped coral reef enclosing a lagoon?

6. What did Aesop write?

7. Which mythical monster has the body, tail and hind legs of a lion and the head, forelegs and wings of an eagle?

8. Which country created the first national netball association?

9. Shere Khan was the villain in which Disney film?

10. Which Great Train Robber played himself in The Sex Pistols' film *The Great Rock 'n' Roll Swindle*?

11. Which actor/singer was plain David Cook before joining the county set?

12. The name of which city in the Middle East means 'warm place'?

13. In which country are the Slieve Bloom mountains?

14. What was Burke and Hare's gruesome pursuit?

15. Who did Brazil's footballers beat 4–1 in the 1970 World Cup Final?

16. What did Beryl call sex in the TV sitcom *The Lovers*?

Answers to page 28
QUIZ 27: **1.** No word in the English language rhymes with them **2.** Noddy **3.** Sicily **4.** Cooking pot **5.** BRM **6.** Lancashire **7.** The Who **8.** St Vitus **9.** Catherine contracted dandruff and didn't want the news to spread **10.** Robin Williams **11.** Murray Walker **12.** Red and white **13.** Thin Lizzy **14.** Two **15.** Smeeta Smitten **16.** Ruud Gullit

Quiz 26

Answers on page 29

1. Susan Sarandon and Geena Davis played which 1991 fugitives?

2. With what sport was David Broome associated?

3. The island of Capri is situated at the southern entrance to which bay?

4. Who performed a concert in the park at the end of each episode of *Trumpton*?

5. Which British political party was founded in 1934?

6. What name is given to the white ball in snooker?

7. What country produces the wine Valpolicella?

8. In which city is the Wailing Wall?

9. What bird can be marsh, coal or crested?

10. What name is given to the President's study in the White House?

11. What is the name of the Marquess of Bath's stately home?

12. Who was the donkey in *Winnie-the-Pooh*?

13. Cheyenne is the capital of which American state?

14. Which group were in *Car Wash* in 1976?

15. Who made snooker's first televised maximum break?

16. What is the favourite coffee shop of the Crane brothers in *Frasier*?

Answers to page 29
QUIZ 28: **1.** 'Twelve plus one' **2.** Havana **3.** 'Mama' Cass Elliot **4.** Henry VI **5.** Set **6.** W.C. Fields **7.** Three **8.** Twiggy **9.** India **10.** Sally Gunnell **11.** Starkiller **12.** Ava Gardner **13.** Bright blue **14.** '19' **15.** Lincolnshire **16.** One

Quiz 27

Answers on page 26

1. What do the words 'month', 'orange', 'silver' and 'purple' have in common?

2. Whose car goes 'parp parp'?

3. From which country does the wine Marsala come?

4. What is a skillet?

5. In what make of car did Graham Hill become Formula One World Champion in 1962?

6. In which English county is the Fylde peninsula?

7. Which band were originally known as The High Numbers?

8. Who is the patron saint of comedians and mental illness?

9. Why did Catherine the Great of Russia have her hairdresser imprisoned in an iron cage for three years?

10. Who played the fast-talking DJ in *Good Morning Vietnam*?

11. Which sports commentator described his last race in September 2001?

12. Which two colours feature on the Austrian flag?

13. Which band sang about *Whisky in the Jar* in 1973?

14. How many Duncans were Kings of Scotland?

15. Who is the 'showbiz kitten' from *Goodness Gracious Me*?

16. Who was the first foreign manager to lift the FA Cup?

Answers to page 26
QUIZ 25: **1.** 22 **2.** Patsy Kensit **3.** Helen Baxendale **4.** Michael Chang **5.** Atoll **6.** Fables **7.** Griffin **8.** New Zealand **9.** *The Jungle Book* **10.** Ronnie Biggs **11.** David Essex **12.** Teheran **13.** Ireland **14.** Body-snatching **15.** Italy **16.** 'Percy Filth'

Quiz 28

Answers on page 27

1. Which sum is an anagram of 'Eleven plus two'?

2. What is the capital of Cuba?

3. Which heavyweight American singer choked to death on a sandwich in 1974?

4. Who became King of England in 1422 at the age of eight months?

5. Of all the words in the English language, which has the most definitions?

6. Which comedy actor's last words, after flicking through the Bible on his deathbed, were: 'I'm looking for a loophole'?

7. How many times did the superstitious Charles Dickens touch everything for luck?

8. Which model had a stint presenting *This Morning* in 2001?

9. The lotus flower is the national symbol of which country?

10. In 1992, which athlete became the first British woman to win an Olympic track gold medal for 28 years?

11. From what was Luke Skywalker's surname in *Star Wars* changed at the last minute because the original sounded too violent?

12. Which movie star, who died in 1990, left her pet corgi Morgan a monthly salary plus his own limo and maid?

13. One in every 5,000 North Atlantic lobsters is born what colour?

14. What number did Paul Hardcastle take to the top of the charts in 1985?

15. In which English county is Louth?

16. How many points are scored for knocking the ball over the crossbar in hurling?

Answers to page 27
QUIZ 26: **1.** *Thelma and Louise* **2.** Show-jumping **3.** Bay of Naples **4.** The fire brigade band **5.** Scottish National Party **6.** Cue ball **7.** Italy **8.** Jerusalem **9.** Tit **10.** The Oval Office **11.** Longleat House **12.** Eeyore **13.** Wyoming **14.** Rose Royce **15.** Steve Davis **16.** Café Nervosa

Quiz 29

Answers on page 32

1. Which famous thespian is the mother of actress Joely Richardson?

2. Lake Tiberias is the modern name for which Biblical sea?

3. Cape Horn is at the southern tip of which group of islands?

4. What does 'ergo' mean in Latin?

5. What is a fieldfare?

6. Who was Queen of England for nine days in 1553?

7. Which spa town at the foot of the Taunus Mountains in Germany gave its name to a soft felt hat for men?

8. Action Man was the British version of which American toy doll?

9. According to medieval Christian legend, what did Jesus drink from at the Last Supper?

10. What is a koto?

11. Which cat was tormented by Pixie and Dixie?

12. Why did the BBC ban Ricky Valance's 1960 hit 'Tell Laura I Love Her'?

13. Which Football League club used to be called New Brompton?

14. What are kurdaitcha shoes – worn by Australian Aborigines – traditionally made from?

15. Leith is the port of which city?

16. How did Herbert Marx get his nickname of 'Zeppo'?

Answers to page 32
QUIZ 31: **1.** Uranus **2.** 16 **3.** Mickey Dolenz **4.** New Zealander **5.** Nero **6.** Liszt **7.** Little Rock **8.** Their fathers were policemen **9.** Blue **10.** Northumberland **11.** The Dagmar **12.** Nene **13.** Australia **14.** Robbie Williams **15.** Germany **16.** 1974

Quiz 30

Answers on page 33

1. What do Ronnie O'Sullivan, Keanu Reeves and Woody Harrelson have in common?

2. Edgbaston cricket ground is in which city?

3. On which island did Steve McGarrett operate?

4. Who wanted to know: 'What's the Frequency, Kenneth?'?

5. In 1953, which jockey finally won his first Epsom Derby at the age of 49?

6. What was installed for the first time at Barclays Bank, Enfield, on 27 June 1967?

7. Richard Hadlee played Test cricket for which country?

8. Which Hollywood actor changed his name from William Franklin Beedle Jnr?

9. What can be the position of a note in the musical scale or a sticky black substance?

10. In which county is the cathedral city of Wells?

11. In which country was the conductor Georg Solti born?

12. Who was the Greek god of dreams?

13. Which British golfer won the US Masters in 1988?

14. Which channel divides Anglesey from the Welsh mainland?

15. Edward Whymper was the first person to climb which Alpine peak?

16. For what is laser an acronym?

Answers to page 33
QUIZ 32: **1.** Tommy Trinder **2.** P. Diddy **3.** Richard **4.** Florence **5.** Tomsk **6.** Malcolm Nash
7. Lincolnshire **8.** Both attended the London School of Economics **9.** George Bernard Shaw **10.** Red
11. Sumo wrestling **12.** Marlene Dietrich ('Marlene on the Wall') **13.** The bra **14.** Belisha beacon
(Sir Leslie Hore-Belisha) **15.** Conner **16.** Crystal Palace

Quiz 31

Answers on page 30

1. Which planet was discovered by William Herschel in 1781?

2. How many weeks did Bryan Adams stay at number one in the UK in 1991 with '(Everything I Do) I Do It For You'?

3. Which of The Monkees once starred in *Circus Boy*?

4. What nationality is former speedway champion Ivan Mauger?

5. Who was said to have fiddled while Rome burned?

6. Who composed 'Transcendental Studies'?

7. What is the state capital of Arkansas?

8. What do Roger Moore, Terry Waite and Julian Clary have in common?

9. What colour does litmus paper turn in the presence of alkali?

10. In which county is Bamburgh Castle?

11. Which wine bar did James Willmott-Brown run in *EastEnders*?

12. Which river flows through Northampton?

13. In which country is the Kakadu National Park?

14. Which rock star famously challenged Liam Gallagher to a fight?

15. The Weimar Republic was established in which country in 1918?

16. In which year did Chris Evert win her first Wimbledon title?

Answers to page 30
QUIZ 29: **1.** Vanessa Redgrave **2.** Sea of Galilee **3.** Tierra del Fuego **4.** Therefore **5.** Bird
6. Lady Jane Grey **7.** Homburg **8.** G.I. Joe **9.** The Holy Grail **10.** A Japanese musical instrument
11. Mr Jinks **12.** It was about death – a taboo subject **13.** Gillingham **14.** Emu feathers
15. Edinburgh **16.** He was born at the time of the first zeppelins

Quiz 32

Answers on page 31

1. Which comedian's catchphrase was 'You lucky people'?

2. To what did Puff Daddy change his name in 2001?

3. What was the name of Hyacinth Bucket's long-suffering husband in *Keeping Up Appearances*?

4. Which city is the capital of the Tuscany region of Italy?

5. Which of the Wombles takes his name from a city in Siberia?

6. Who was the Glamorgan bowler when Nottinghamshire's Gary Sobers established a world record by hitting six sixes in one over at Swansea in 1968?

7. In which county is the resort of Ingoldmells?

8. Which seat of learning links Mick Jagger and John F. Kennedy?

9. Who wrote *Arms and the Man* and *Man and Superman*?

10. What colour beak does a shelduck have?

11. What is the national sport of Japan?

12. Which movie star was the subject of a 1986 song by Suzanne Vega?

13. What garment did Mary Phelps Jacob (aka Mrs Caresse Crosby) perfect in 1913?

14. Which flashing road safety innovation of 1934 was named after the minister of transport at the time?

15. What was the family surname in *Roseanne*?

16. Steve Bruce was appointed manager of which London football club in the summer of 2001?

Answers to page 31
QUIZ 30: **1.** Their fathers have all served jail sentences **2.** Birmingham **3.** Hawaii (*Hawaii Five-0*) **4.** R.E.M. **5.** Sir Gordon Richards **6.** Cash dispenser **7.** New Zealand **8.** William Holden **9.** Pitch **10.** Somerset **11.** Hungary **12.** Morpheus **13.** Sandy Lyle **14.** Menai Strait **15.** Matterhorn **16.** Light Amplification by Stimulated Emission of Radiation

Quiz 33

Answers on page 36

1. Which is the second largest planet in the solar system?

2. Philip Pirrip is the central character in which Dickens novel?

3. Which four countries share borders with Italy?

4. Which sea separates Vietnam from the Philippines?

5. Who played Mary Jane to Tobey Maguire's Spider-man in 2002?

6. Which two Davids led the Liberal-SDP alliance of the 1980s?

7. What is the trade name for polytetrafluoroethene?

8. Which Israeli city gives its name to a type of orange?

9. Which football club played at Anfield before Liverpool?

10. Who directed *This Is Spinal Tap* and *When Harry Met Sally*?

11. In which year was 'Love Me for a Reason' a UK number one for The Osmonds?

12. Who did Billy Wilder say had 'breasts like granite and a brain like Swiss cheese'?

13. Who played the title role in the film *Shirley Valentine*?

14. Which French jockey won the 1998 Epsom Derby on High Rise?

15. What is a whippoorwill?

16. From which Yorkshire port did Captain Cook sail in the *Resolution* on his 1768 voyage to the Pacific?

Answers to page 36
QUIZ 35: **1.** 'My Way' **2.** Richard Hannon **3.** *Jane Eyre* **4.** Yellow no-parking lines **5.** 1982 **6.** One-pound coins **7.** Bear **8.** Cambridge's run of seven wins in a row **9.** The Bee Gees **10.** Kroner **11.** Lifting machinery on a ship **12.** George Eliot **13.** Emily's **14.** Paul Weller **15.** *Women in Love* **16.** Green

Quiz 34

Answers on page 37

1. Who wrote *Rebecca*?

2. Which stretch of water separates Edinburgh from Fife?

3. Boavista play their football in which country?

4. As whom was William Simmonite better known in a long-running BBC sitcom?

5. Findus is an abbreviation of the name of which Swedish company?

6. The name of which Central American capital city means 'holy saviour'?

7. In which cathedral was Thomas à Becket murdered?

8. In which ship did Francis Drake sail around the world?

9. Dresden is the capital of which German state?

10. On which race track is the Champion Hurdle run?

11. What is a female rabbit called?

12. Who wrote the stories of *Thomas the Tank Engine*?

13. What is a merganser?

14. Where were The Police walking in 1979?

15. In 1993, which horse won the Grand National that never was?

16. Nancy Wilkinson was the first winner of which TV title in 1972?

Answers to page 37
QUIZ 36: **1.** Farnborough **2.** Lucinda Prior-Palmer **3.** Australian **4.** Audrey fforbes-Hamilton
5. Samuel Crompton **6.** Rhine **7.** Nutmeggers **8.** Hungary **9.** Will Smith **10.** 1955 **11.** Liberia
12. Wiltshire **13.** Edward VI **14.** Al Martino **15.** Bolton Wanderers **16.** Duke of Edinburgh

Quiz 35

Answers on page 34

1. Which record did Sir David Frost, Geoffrey Boycott and Johnny Speight all choose on *Desert Island Discs*?

2. Which racehorse trainer used to be a drummer with The Troggs?

3. Edward Rochester featured in which Charlotte Brontë novel?

4. What did Slough acquire in 1956 that no other British town had?

5. In which year was Prince William born?

6. What were introduced to the British currency in 1983?

7. What kind of animal was Gentle Ben?

8. What sequence was broken by Oxford in the 2000 University Boat Race?

9. Which internationally successful pop brothers were born on the Isle of Man?

10. What is the currency of Denmark?

11. What is a derrick?

12. What was the pen name of author Mary Ann Evans?

13. In whose shop window did Bagpuss sit?

14. Whose 1995 album was titled *Stanley Road*?

15. For which film did Glenda Jackson win an Academy Award for Best Actress in 1970?

16. What colour is emerald?

Answers to page 34

QUIZ 33: **1.** Saturn **2.** *Great Expectations* **3.** France, Switzerland, Austria and Slovenia **4.** South China Sea **5.** Kirsten Dunst **6.** Steel and Owen **7.** Teflon **8.** Jaffa **9.** Everton **10.** Rob Reiner **11.** 1974 **12.** Marilyn Monroe **13.** Pauline Collins **14.** Olivier Peslier **15.** A bird **16.** Whitby

Quiz 36

Answers on page 35

1. Which Hampshire town is famous for its air show?

2. What was the maiden name of British three-day eventer Lucinda Green?

3. What nationality is feminist Germaine Greer?

4. Who did Penelope Keith play in *To the Manor Born*?

5. Whose mule was a key invention during the Industrial Revolution?

6. Which river is straddled by the Bendorf Bridge at Coblenz?

7. What are inhabitants of Connecticut known as?

8. Who were the first non-British football nation to defeat England at Wembley?

9. Who reached number one in 1997 with 'Men in Black'?

10. In which year was James Dean killed in a car crash?

11. Monrovia is the capital of which country?

12. In which county is Stonehenge?

13. Who succeeded Henry VIII as King of England?

14. Who had the first-ever UK number one single?

15. Which football club plays at the Reebok Stadium?

16. What was Edmund's title in the first series of *Blackadder*?

Answers to page 35
QUIZ 34: **1.** Daphne du Maurier **2.** Firth of Forth **3.** Portugal **4.** 'Compo' **5.** Fruit Industries **6.** San Salvador **7.** Canterbury **8.** *Golden Hind* **9.** Saxony **10.** Cheltenham **11.** Doe **12.** Rev. W. Awdry **13.** A type of duck **14.** On the moon **15.** Esha Ness **16.** *Mastermind*

Quiz 37

Answers on page 40

1. Which building on the River Jumna near Agra was constructed by 20,000 workmen?

2. Which actress starred in *There's Something About Mary* and *Being John Malkovich*?

3. What nationality is James Last?

4. What is special about the echidna and the duck-billed platypus?

5. Where did Rosie and Jim live?

6. Where would you find futtock plates?

7. Qantas is the national airline of which country?

8. Which French oceanographer commanded the boat *Calypso*?

9. Which Belgian tennis player got to the final of the Wimbledon ladies' singles in 2001?

10. Which actor, famous for playing a TV soap thug, was voted Rector of Glasgow University in 1999?

11. In which African country is the city of Constantine?

12. Who wrote *Hedda Gabler*?

13. Which Australian squash player won the British Women's Open title a record 16 years in succession from 1962 to 1977?

14. Which Premiership football club plays at the Riverside Stadium?

15. Francisco Lopez was a 19th-century dictator of which South American country?

16. How many points is the letter 'X' worth in Scrabble?

Answers to page 40
QUIZ 39: **1.** 64 **2.** Sigmund Freud **3.** Walton **4.** State Earnings-Related Pension Schemes **5.** Terry-Thomas **6.** Yo-yo **7.** It is the smallest house in Britain **8.** Botswana **9.** Millwall **10.** 1984 **11.** A musical instrument **12.** Swedish **13.** Preston Sturges **14.** Styx **15.** The Mediterranean **16.** Haircut 100

Quiz 38

Answers on page 41

1. Birmingham Bullets and Leicester Riders are teams in which sport?

2. Shirley Manson is the singer with which band?

3. Which cricketer was dropped after flying a Tiger Moth during a match on the 1991 tour of Australia?

4. What is the name of the clown on *The Simpsons*?

5. Which country makes Nokia mobile phones?

6. Which animated children's TV series featured the Hemulen?

7. Which former chairman of British Rail is the namesake of *Spiderman*'s alter ego?

8. Which is the oldest bridge across the River Seine in Paris?

9. What pen name was used by writer Eric Arthur Blair?

10. What does UNESCO stand for?

11. What is a sequoia?

12. Aurora borealis are otherwise known as what?

13. Who plays Waynetta Slob to Harry Enfield's Wayne?

14. What did Englishman Harry Brearley invent in 1913?

15. Which car manufacturing company was named after the ten-year-old daughter of Austrian financier and motor-racing enthusiast Emil Jellinek?

16. Which boxer was nicknamed 'The Louisville Lip'?

Answers to page 41
QUIZ 40: **1.** Dodo **2.** Chaka Khan **3.** Newmarket **4.** South Pole **5.** The badger parade **6.** Honeysuckle **7.** Strand **8.** Italy **9.** East Sussex **10.** Duran Duran **11.** Kamikaze **12.** Mercury **13.** Lusaka **14.** Show-jumping **15.** Olive Oyl **16.** Cloud

Quiz 39

Answers on page 38

1. How many squares are there on a draughts board?

2. Which Austrian physician pioneered the study of the unconscious mind?

3. Which Essex resort is 'on the Naze'?

4. Of what is SERPS an acronym?

5. On which British comedy actor was Basil Brush's voice based?

6. Which child's game was developed from a Filipino weapon?

7. What is special about a 19th-century fisherman's cottage on the quay at Conwy, North Wales?

8. Which country has the highest percentage of female heads of household in the world?

9. Who were the first Third Division club to reach the semi-finals of the FA Cup?

10. In which year did George Michael reach number one in the UK with 'Careless Whisper'?

11. What is a dulcimer?

12. What nationality was the playwright August Strindberg?

13. To what did US film director and writer Edmond Biden change his name?

14. In Greek mythology, which river surrounded the underworld?

15. Which sea did the Romans refer to as 'mare nostrum'?

16. Which band sang about their 'Favourite Shirts' in 1981?

Answers to page 38
QUIZ 37: **1.** Taj Mahal **2.** Cameron Diaz **3.** German **4.** They are the world's only egg-laying mammals **5.** On a canal boat **6.** On a ship **7.** Australia **8.** Jacques Cousteau **9.** Justine Henin **10.** Ross Kemp (Grant Mitchell) **11.** Algeria **12.** Henrik Ibsen **13.** Heather McKay **14.** Middlesbrough **15.** Paraguay **16.** Eight

Quiz 40

Answers on page 39

1. Which extinct bird's name is Dutch for 'fat bum'?

2. Whose first UK hit was 'I'm Every Woman'?

3. On which racecourse is the One Thousand Guineas run?

4. What was Roald Amundsen the first person to reach?

5. Harry Hill was distraught to see which parade repeatedly cancelled?

6. What is another name for a woodbine when it grows in your garden?

7. According to the TV commercials, which cigarette were you never alone with?

8. Which footballing country won the 1982 World Cup?

9. In which English county is Ashdown Forest?

10. Which eighties band released the album *Seven and the Ragged Tiger*?

11. Which Japanese military word means 'divine wind'?

12. Hg is the chemical symbol for which element?

13. What is the capital of Zambia?

14. At which sport did Richard Meade represent his country?

15. Which damsel-in-distress has vital statistics of 19-19-19?

16. Cumulus and cirrus are types of what?

Answers to page 39
QUIZ 38: **1.** Basketball **2.** Garbage **3.** David Gower **4.** Krusty **5.** Finland **6.** *The Moomins* **7.** Peter Parker **8.** Pont Neuf **9.** George Orwell **10.** United Nations Educational, Scientific and Cultural Organisation **11.** A redwood tree **12.** The northern lights **13.** Kathy Burke **14.** Stainless steel **15.** Mercedes **16.** Muhammad Ali

Quiz 41

Answers on page 44

1. Which Second Division football club paid £1.7 million for Stoke City striker Peter Thorne in 2001?

2. Which TV series featured a computer-generated dancing baby named Mr Huggy?

3. On which river does the Argentine city of Corrientes stand?

4. Which island is situated due north of Sardinia?

5. What sport takes place at the Daytona circuit in the USA?

6. Paul Keating was Prime Minister of which country from 1991 to 1996?

7. Which bird had a UK number one hit in 1972?

8. Which was the first frozen food to go on sale in Britain?

9. Which prototype took 12 minutes to boil?

10. What can be a colourful crow or a decorating tool?

11. A scene showing which naked area of Sylvia Sidney's body when she embraced Cary Grant was cut by the Japanese from the 1932 movie *Madame Butterfly*?

12. Which actor was born Coy Luther Perry III but chose his stage name from his favourite movie, *Cool Hand Luke*?

13. Which venomous snake is thought to be responsible for more human deaths than any other?

14. Which world championships take place each year at the Corner Pin public house at Ramsbottom near Manchester?

15. How many degrees are there in a circle?

16. What nationality was the composer Delius?

Answers to page 44
QUIZ 43: **1.** It was composed entirely of Scots **2.** A tropical vine **3.** James Boswell **4.** Duke of Gloucester **5.** A seabird **6.** His boomerang **7.** Queen **8.** Loganberry **9.** Mountaineering **10.** A fearless Viking warrior **11.** The Alamo **12.** Homer **13.** Jonathan Aitken **14.** Ken Matthews **15.** John Hurt **16.** *Home to Roost*

Quiz 42

Answers on page 45

1. The town of Llanberis is at the foot of which mountain?

2. In *This Sporting Life*, Richard Harris played a miner convinced that his future lay in which sport?

3. What is the opposite of an anode?

4. Cauliflower is a variety of which vegetable?

5. Which wild Northumberland family were distinguishable by the grey streak in their hair?

6. What is the capital of Brazil?

7. Which progressive rock band released the albums *Fragile* and *Close to the Edge*?

8. As what is sodium hydroxide otherwise known?

9. In which American state is Sacramento?

10. Which TV show features 'Dictionary Corner'?

11. Which French engineer was responsible for the construction of the Suez Canal?

12. Former Olympic marathon champion Abebe Bikila represented which country?

13. In 1997, which band appealed 'Help the Aged'?

14. Which Hollywood star changed his name from John Carter?

15. Which Argentine golfer lost out on the 1968 US Masters after his playing partner accidentally put down the wrong score for a hole?

16. Which card game was first played among members of the Indian Civil Service around 1900?

Answers to page 45
QUIZ 44: **1.** Cockfosters **2.** *The Taming of the Shrew* **3.** West Indies **4.** Joe Meek **5.** Airdrie **6.** Chief Robert T. Ironside **7.** Blue and white **8.** France **9.** Nepal **10.** Andrew **11.** Snooker **12.** Plymouth **13.** Baseball **14.** Denmark **15.** Morecambe and Wise **16.** Anchorage

Quiz 43

Answers on page 42

1. What was remarkable about the team fielded by Accrington Stanley for a 1955 Football League match?

2. What is bougainvillea?

3. Who was Dr Samuel Johnson's biographer?

4. What was Richard III's title before he became king?

5. What is a booby?

6. What wouldn't come back for Charlie Drake?

7. John Deacon and Roger Taylor were members of which band?

8. Which fruit is named after an American judge who crossed a wild blackberry with a cultivated raspberry?

9. What is Chris Bonington's favourite pursuit?

10. Who was berserker?

11. At which battle was Davy Crockett killed?

12. Who wrote the *Iliad*?

13. Which former Conservative minister was jailed for 18 months in 1999 for perjury and perverting the course of justice?

14. Which Briton won gold at the 1964 Olympics in the 20km walk?

15. Who starred in the film of *The Elephant Man*?

16. Which sitcom starred John Thaw as Henry Willows?

Answers to page 42
QUIZ 41: **1.** Cardiff City **2.** *Ally McBeal* **3.** Parana **4.** Corsica **5.** Motor-racing **6.** Australia **7.** Lieutenant Pigeon **8.** Asparagus **9.** The electric kettle **10.** Roller **11.** Her left elbow **12.** Luke Perry **13.** Carpet viper **14.** The World Black Pudding Knocking Championships **15.** 360 **16.** English

Quiz 44

Answers on page 43

1. Which station stands at the northern end of London Underground's Piccadilly Line?

2. The 1999 movie *10 Things I Hate About You* was an update of which Shakespeare play?

3. For which country does Brian Lara play Test cricket?

4. Which record producer shot himself dead on 3 February 1967, the anniversary of the death of his hero, Buddy Holly?

5. Which Scottish football club used to be known as Excelsior FC?

6. Which TV detective was confined to a wheelchair?

7. What two colours feature on the Greek national flag?

8. Which country is the most popular destination with foreign tourists?

9. In which country is Mount Everest?

10. What is the Christian name of the singer Roachford?

11. In which game would you use a 'spider'?

12. The River Tamar flows into the sea at which port?

13. At what sport was Babe Ruth a national hero?

14. Aalborg is a port in which country?

15. Bartholomew and Wiseman became better known as which duo?

16. What is the largest town in Alaska?

Answers to page 43
QUIZ 42: **1.** Snowdon **2.** Rugby League **3.** Cathode **4.** Cabbage **5.** *The Mallens* **6.** Brasilia **7.** Yes **8.** Caustic soda **9.** California **10.** *Countdown* **11.** Ferdinand de Lesseps **12.** Ethiopia **13.** Pulp **14.** Charlton Heston **15.** Roberto De Vicenzo **16.** Bridge

Quiz 45

Answers on page 48

1. Who wrote the screenplay of *Four Weddings and a Funeral*?

2. Who was the only man who could ever reach Dusty Springfield?

3. Which Liverpool couple had sextuplets in 1983?

4. Which Beatle played a lavatory attendant in a sketch on *Not Only...But Also* with Peter Cook and Dudley Moore?

5. Which Football League club left the Manor Ground for good in 2001?

6. Jonathan and Jennifer were which seventies crime-fighting husband-and-wife team?

7. On which of the Great Lakes is Chicago a port?

8. In Greek legend, which king was granted the gift of converting all he touched to gold?

9. Which planet is closest to the Sun?

10. Who went from drinking Gold Blend to starring in *Buffy the Vampire Slayer*?

11. Paul Jones was replaced by Mike D'Abo as singer with which sixties band?

12. What is the capital of Saxony?

13. Which city used to be called Constantinople?

14. In 2001, which country won the Eurovision Song Contest for the first time?

15. Which James Bond used to work as a French polisher for a coffin-maker?

16. What were the names of aviation pioneers the Wright brothers?

Answers to page 48
QUIZ 47: **1.** Arthur Daley **2.** Fulham **3.** Frederick Forsyth **4.** A small bird **5.** The inert gases **6.** Rita Hayworth **7.** Bob the Builder **8.** James I **9.** Dennis **10.** Algeria **11.** Slade **12.** Toaster **13.** New York **14.** Yellow **15.** Portuguese **16.** Violin

Quiz 46

Answers on page 49

1. Which US President was known as 'The Bull Moose'?

2. Which Miss Teenage Memphis 1966 went on to star in her own TV sitcom?

3. Which Hollywood heart-throb of the 1930s was listed on his birth certificate as a girl?

4. In which country is the Tysee waterfall?

5. Where will the 2004 Olympic Games be held?

6. Who wrote *Gulliver's Travels*?

7. Which US actor was born Bernard Schwarz?

8. What did Kim Cotton become in 1985?

9. Which band used to be called Seymour?

10. As whom is Edson Arantes do Nascimento better known?

11. Who was known as the Iron Duke?

12. Who won *Celebrity Big Brother* in 2002?

13. What is the currency of Thailand?

14. What is Margaret Thatcher's middle name?

15. Who became US President following the assassination of Kennedy?

16. In which car did Damon Hill win the Formula One World Drivers' Championship?

Answers to page 49
QUIZ 48: **1.** 1839 **2.** Hertfordshire **3.** Identikits **4.** Tara King **5.** Bette Davis **6.** A poisonous plant **7.** Edward II **8.** The Kilshaws **9.** Ethiopia **10.** Travis **11.** Suva **12.** Henry Fielding **13.** Red **14.** Sloths **15.** Lily **16.** Ontario

Quiz 47

Answers on page 46

1. Who promised: 'The world is your lobster'?

2. The owner of Harrods is also the chairman of which Premiership football club?

3. Who wrote *The Day of the Jackal*?

4. What is a dunnock?

5. Helium, neon, argon, krypton, xenon and radon are collectively known as what?

6. Which Hollywood star of the 1940s was born Margarita Carmen Cansino?

7. Wendy, Scoop, Muck and Dizzy are friends of whom?

8. Who was the first Stuart King of England?

9. Which boy's name is derived from Dionysus, the Greek god of wine?

10. DZ is the international vehicle index mark for which country?

11. Don Powell was the drummer with which seventies band?

12. Which kitchen appliance was invented by the American Charles Strite in 1927?

13. In which city would you cross the Verrazano Narrows Suspension Bridge?

14. What colour are the flowers of a forsythia?

15. What nationality was the footballer Eusebio?

16. With what musical instrument is Stephane Grappelli primarily associated?

Answers to page 46
QUIZ 45: **1.** Richard Curtis **2.** 'Son of a Preacher Man' **3.** The Waltons **4.** John Lennon **5.** Oxford United **6.** *Hart to Hart* **7.** Michigan **8.** Midas **9.** Mercury **10.** Anthony Head **11.** Manfred Mann **12.** Dresden **13.** Istanbul **14.** Estonia **15.** Sean Connery **16.** Orville and Wilbur

Quiz 48

Answers on page 47

1. In which year was the Grand National first run?

2. In which county is Hemel Hempstead?

3. What were introduced for the first time by Scotland Yard in 1961?

4. Which of Steed's sidekicks in *The Avengers* was played by Linda Thorson?

5. Who said: 'The best time I ever had with Joan Crawford was when I pushed her down the stairs in *Whatever Happened to Baby Jane*'?

6. What is henbane?

7. Which English king was murdered in Berkeley Castle?

8. Which British couple were at the centre of a storm in 2000 over their attempts to procure a baby over the Internet?

9. Of which country did Haile Selassie become emperor in 1930?

10. Which band released the album *The Man Who*?

11. What is the capital of the Republic of Fiji?

12. Which English novelist's best-known work was *Tom Jones*?

13. According to Dutch superstition, people with what colour hair bring bad luck?

14. Which animals move so slowly that algae grow in their hair?

15. The onion is a member of which family?

16. The Niagara Falls are located in which Canadian province?

Answers to page 47
QUIZ 46: **1.** Theodore Roosevelt **2.** Cybill Shepherd **3.** Clark Gable **4.** Norway **5.** Athens
6. Jonathan Swift **7.** Tony Curtis **8.** Britain's first commercial surrogate mother **9.** Blur **10.** Pele
11. The Duke of Wellington **12.** Mark Owen **13.** Baht **14.** Hilda **15.** Lyndon B. Johnson **16.** Williams

Quiz 49

Answers on page 52

1. Which British motor-racing team was launched by Tony Vandervell?

2. Which communications satellite was launched in 1962 to provide the first live TV transmissions between the USA and Europe?

3. Which T is one of the six counties of Northern Ireland?

4. What type of geographical feature is Skiddaw?

5. Which movie star, who separated in 2001 from his wife, was once voted Least Likely To Succeed by his classmates?

6. Which board game was the brainchild of Chris and John Haney and Scott Abbott?

7. What is a siskin?

8. Renée Zellweger and Hugh Grant starred in which Helen Fielding adaptation?

9. Which Quasimodo won the Nobel Prize for Literature in 1959?

10. In 1986, 13-year-old Sandra Kim won the Eurovision Song Contest for which country?

11. In football, which country staged the 1958 World Cup finals?

12. Au is the chemical symbol for which element?

13. What does 'décolleté' mean in the fashion world?

14. Who is the chief god in Scandinavian mythology?

15. At which London railway station would you arrive if travelling from Swindon?

16. What was special about the televised football match between Liverpool and West Ham on 15 November 1969?

Answers to page 52
QUIZ 51: **1.** Monsoon **2.** Bob Hawke **3.** Sweden **4.** Morpeth **5.** LXXX **6.** 14 **7.** Kuala Lumpur **8.** Malawi **9.** Each have eyes of different colours **10.** REO Speedwagon **11.** Ireland **12.** Calais **13.** Hooghly **14.** Jane Tennison **15.** Russell Crowe **16.** Mia Farrow

Quiz 50

Answers on page 53

1. Justine Frischmann, Janet Street-Porter and Queen Noor of Jordan all studied to be what?

2. What was the name of Boycie's wife in *Only Fools and Horses*?

3. Which Football League club started the 2001–2 season playing home matches at Dorchester Town?

4. Which pen name did R.C. Lamburn use to create the adventures of a mischievous schoolboy?

5. Which duo were first to utter the corny line: 'If I Said You Have A Beautiful Body Would You Hold It Against Me'?

6. What flower is ling more commonly known as?

7. For which country does footballer Dan Petrescu play?

8. What is the female singer's equivalent of an alto voice?

9. Ownership of Jutland is divided between which two countries?

10. Arthur Stanley Jefferson achieved fame as which half of a comic duo?

11. Ascunción is the capital of which South American country?

12. Which bubble threatened to destroy the British economy in the 18th century?

13. Racehorse No Bombs was disqualified after winning a race at Ascot for eating what on the way to the races?

14. In which country was Lego invented?

15. What foodstuff was originally called an Eskimo Pie?

16. What is a liger?

Answers to page 53
QUIZ 52: **1.** Bernie the Bolt **2.** Sarah Tisdall **3.** Richard **4.** Derbyshire, South Yorkshire, Lincolnshire and Leicestershire **5.** Supergrass **6.** Iran **7.** Australia **8.** The zip **9.** The Nile **10.** Montevideo **11.** Brian Conley **12.** Germany **13.** Hereward the Wake **14.** Ernest Hemingway **15.** Hendon **16.** Plaster of Paris

Quiz 51

Answers on page 50

1. What is Edina's surname in *Absolutely Fabulous*?

2. Who was Prime Minister of Australia from 1983 to 1991?

3. Which Scandinavian country's flag is a yellow cross on a blue background?

4. Which town is the administrative centre of Northumberland?

5. What is 80 in Roman numerals?

6. How many pounds are there in a stone?

7. Which city houses the two Petronas skyscrapers, currently the tallest buildings in the world?

8. Which African country used to be called Nyasaland?

9. Which physical trait is shared by Jane Seymour and David Bowie?

10. Which US group took their name from a fire engine?

11. Which country's rugby union team plays at Lansdowne Road?

12. Which port did the French regain from English control in 1558?

13. On which river does Calcutta stand?

14. Which police officer did Helen Mirren play in *Prime Suspect*?

15. Who was the Antipodean star of the movie *Gladiator*?

16. The sister of which actress was the subject of The Beatles' 'Dear Prudence'?

Answers to page 50
QUIZ 49: **1.** Vanwall **2.** *Telstar* **3.** Tyrone **4.** A mountain (in the Lake District) **5.** Tom Cruise **6.** Trivial Pursuit **7.** A bird **8.** *Bridget Jones's Diary* **9.** Salvatore Quasimodo **10.** Belgium **11.** Sweden **12.** Gold **13.** Low cut **14.** Odin **15.** Paddington **16.** It was the first TV game in colour

Quiz 52

Answers on page 51

1. Who loaded the crossbows on *The Golden Shot*?

2. Which Foreign Office clerk was jailed in 1984 for passing Cruise missile documents to the *Guardian*?

3. Which son of Oliver Cromwell succeeded him as Lord Protector?

4. Which four counties border Nottinghamshire?

5. Gaz Coombes is the singer with which band?

6. In which country are the ruins of Persepolis?

7. Which country has won most Commonwealth Games gold medals?

8. What was invented by Whitcomb L. Judson in 1893?

9. Which is the longest river in the world?

10. The name of which South American capital city means 'I see the mountain'?

11. Which British comedian and chat show host had 'No Entry' tattooed on his bottom?

12. Quark is which country's most popular cheese?

13. Who led a revolt against the Normans in 1070 from his stronghold on the Isle of Ely?

14. Who wrote *The Old Man and the Sea*?

15. Where is the Metropolitan Police Training School?

16. What is burned gypsum otherwise known as?

Answers to page 51
QUIZ 50: **1.** Architects **2.** Marlene **3.** Bournemouth **4.** Richmal Crompton (*Just William*) **5.** Bellamy Brothers **6.** Heather **7.** Romania **8.** Contralto **9.** Denmark and Germany **10.** Stan Laurel **11.** Paraguay **12.** South Sea Bubble **13.** Mars Bar **14.** Denmark **15.** Choc ice **16.** The offspring of a lion and tigress

Quiz 53

Answers on page 56

1. Which letter of the English alphabet hasn't changed shape since its introduction around 130 BC?

2. The pips of which fruit contain a minute measure of cyanide?

3. Why don't bulls see red?

4. Which former member of the band was the subject of Pink Floyd's 'Shine On You Crazy Diamond'?

5. What is the fourth letter of the Greek alphabet?

6. What is the highest that can be scored with a single dart?

7. What was the name of Lenny Henry's Chef?

8. What was the first name of the French philosopher and mathematician Descartes?

9. Who once wrote three symphonies in the space of six weeks?

10. Whose run of three successive UK number one singles was interrupted by St Winifred's School Choir with 'There's No One Quite Like Grandma'?

11. Which football manager tried to lead his team off the pitch before a penalty shoot-out in a play-off match at the end of the 2000–1 season?

12. What is the state capital of Australia's Northern Territory?

13. Who wrote the Barchester series of novels?

14. Which musical instrument has an inner sliding tube?

15. TB is an abbreviation for which disease?

16. Who did Mordred call 'uncle Arthur'?

Answers to page 56
QUIZ 55: **1.** The Cruisers **2.** Berkshire **3.** Dinar **4.** Radius **5.** Gulliver **6.** 40 **7.** Germany, Austria, Liechtenstein, Italy and France **8.** Sandy Lyle **9.** Maplins **10.** Peter Frampton **11.** Sylvester Stallone **12.** Syria **13.** *Who Wants To Be a Millionaire* **14.** Synonym **15.** Lilac **16.** It is the most northerly point on the British mainland

Quiz 54

Answers on page 57

1. Whose film crew were accused of harassing Prince William at the start of his first university term?

2. What is the American equivalent of British Summer Time?

3. Which American golfer won the 2001 USPGA tournament?

4. Which English aircraft designer and manufacturer produced the Tiger Moth and the Mosquito?

5. From which continent do piranha fish come?

6. Which insect saw Cock Robin die?

7. Who started his acting career as The Fresh Prince of Bel-Air?

8. Which small stringed instrument takes its name from the Hawaiian for 'jumping flea'?

9. Which is the only Great Lake situated entirely within the United States?

10. Which song links Millie and Bad Manners?

11. In which English county is Launceston?

12. As whom is Steveland Judkins better known?

13. Which soldier, who conquered Sicily and Naples in 1860, gave his name to a type of biscuit?

14. What part of the body is affected by periodontal disease?

15. The Green Goblin is the arch enemy of which superhero?

16. Which Austrian skier won a record 25 World Cup downhill events from 1974 to 1984?

Answers to page 57
QUIZ 56: **1.** A type of cheese **2.** Climb trees **3.** Van Gogh **4.** They are the only words in the English language where the five vowels are in alphabetical order **5.** Phil Neville **6.** The Yardbirds **7.** Iceland **8.** Tarzan (Lincoln stabbed a lion that attacked him) **9.** Japan **10.** Shinty **11.** Strasbourg **12.** Bay of Biscay **13.** Madonna **14.** Sylvester Stallone **15.** Both were once postmen **16.** 'It's Like That'

Quiz 55

Answers on page 54

1. What was the name of Dave Berry's backing group?

2. In which English county is the Royal Military Academy, Sandhurst?

3. Which currency is used by Jordan, Iraq and Libya?

4. What is the name for a line drawn from the centre of a circle to the circumference?

5. Who visited Lilliput and Brobdingnag?

6. According to legend, for how many days is the weather on St Swithun's Day set to continue?

7. Which five countries border Switzerland?

8. In 1985, who became the first British golfer to win the Open for 16 years?

9. What was the name of the holiday camp in *Hi-De-Hi!*?

10. Who fronted a band called Camel?

11. Which Hollywood star is known as the 'Italian Stallion'?

12. Aleppo and Homs are towns in which Middle East country?

13. Major Charles Ingram's jackpot win on which TV quiz was found to be fraudulent?

14. What is the name for two words with the same meaning?

15. Which sweetly scented tree has the Latin name *Syringa vulgaris*?

16. What is the geographical significance of Dunnet Head in Scotland?

Answers to page 54
QUIZ 53: **1.** 0 **2.** Apples **3.** They're colour-blind **4.** Syd Barrett **5.** Delta **6.** 60 **7.** Gareth Blackstock **8.** René **9.** Mozart **10.** John Lennon **11.** Trevor Francis (Birmingham City) **12.** Darwin **13.** Anthony Trollope **14.** Trombone **15.** Tuberculosis **16.** King Arthur

Quiz 56

Answers on page 55

1. What is Blue Vinny?

2. What can robber crabs do that other crabs can't?

3. Which artist painted a picture a day for the last 70 days of his life?

4. What do the words 'abstemious', 'abstentious', 'arsenious', 'arteriosus' and 'facetious' have in common?

5. Who gave away a late penalty to put England out of the 2000 European Championship finals?

6. Keith Relf was lead singer with which sixties band?

7. Which country publishes more books per head than any other in the world?

8. What role was Elmo Lincoln playing when he stabbed his co-star to death while filming a 1918 movie?

9. In which country is Mount Fuji?

10. Which game uses a curved stick called a caman?

11. Which French city stands on the River Ill?

12. Which stretch of water used to be called the Gulf of Gascony?

13. Which singer played the part of a fencing instructor in *Die Another Day*?

14. Who walked out on the 1985 movie *Beverly Hills Cop* after his demand for more action scenes was rejected?

15. What job links Abraham Lincoln and Rock Hudson?

16. What was the title of the 1998 number one for Run DMC vs Jason Nevins?

Answers to page 55
QUIZ 54: **1.** Prince Edward **2.** Daylight Saving Time **3.** David Toms **4.** Geoffrey de Havilland **5.** South America **6.** The fly **7.** Will Smith **8.** Ukelele **9.** Lake Michigan **10.** 'My Boy Lollipop' **11.** Cornwall **12.** Stevie Wonder **13.** Garibaldi **14.** Gums **15.** Spiderman **16.** Franz Klammer

Quiz 57

Answers on page 60

1. Who were the first club to score 1,000 Football League goals?

2. Who starred in *Breakfast at Tiffany's* and *My Fair Lady*?

3. What nationality was playwright Samuel Beckett?

4. Which foodstuff was invented by Frenchman Hippolyte Mège-Mouries in 1868?

5. What is the chemical symbol for iron?

6. Which European country has the international vehicle index mark CH?

7. Which boy's name means 'small' in Latin?

8. What is the capital of Uzbekistan?

9. Who sang about a 'Stupid Girl' in 1996?

10. And who did Captain Mainwaring think was a 'stupid boy'?

11. Which town is the administrative centre of Essex?

12. What is the name of an otter's home?

13. Which camp TV presenter was named after the tough-guy actor who starred in *Tales of Wells Fargo*?

14. Dar es Salaam is the chief seaport in which country?

15. Which Australian golfer won the British Open in 1991?

16. Which is the world's largest inland sea?

Answers to page 60
QUIZ 59: **1.** *The Color of Money* **2.** Alfred **3.** Bayeux Tapestry **4.** Montrose **5.** Thermos flask
6. North Sea **7.** Liverpool **8.** Bangladesh **9.** Pat Eddery **10.** John Adams **11.** Supermarket
12. A small whirlpool **13.** Catkins **14.** Derek Fowlds (*The Basil Brush Show* to *Yes, Minister*)
15. Eldred **16.** Lynn Davies and Mary Rand

Quiz 58

Answers on page 61

1. Which former England football manager was named after an ill-fated bandleader?

2. Britney Spears appeared in which TV series about a girl with supernatural powers?

3. *Saintpaulia* is the Latin name for which popular house plant?

4. Which musical instrument was invented by Cyrill Damien in 1829?

5. Who directed *Dances With Wolves*?

6. Which country used to be called Kampuchea?

7. Georgetown is the capital of which South American country?

8. In which year was the Gunpowder Plot?

9. Who was head of the Gestapo from 1936?

10. For which county did Len Hutton play cricket?

11. A gumtree is the common name for which tree?

12. In which county is Caernarvon?

13. What is the state capital of Idaho?

14. Which Belgian punk had a 1978 hit with 'Ça Plane Pour Moi'?

15. With what physical handicap was Dudley Moore born?

16. Which comedian's real name is Jim Moir?

Answers to page 61
QUIZ 60: **1.** Violet **2.** Green, white and orange **3.** Four – France, The Netherlands, Germany and Luxembourg **4.** Peter Dimmock **5.** Paul Nicholas **6.** Subbuteo (*Falco subbuteo* is the Latin name for the hobby) **7.** Haiti **8.** Hercule Poirot **9.** The Thompson Twins **10.** Ben Kingsley **11.** The Oaks **12.** *Henry VIII* **13.** Stephen Fry **14.** Fencing **15.** A small flute **16.** Greek

Quiz 59

Answers on page 58

1. For which film did Paul Newman win an Oscar for Best Actor in 1986?

2. What is the name of Batman's butler?

3. Which tapestry gives a vivid pictorial record of the Norman Conquest?

4. Which Scottish League football team are nicknamed the 'Gable Endies'?

5. What type of flask was originally called a Dewar Vessel in honour of its inventor?

6. The Dogger Bank is a submerged sandbank in which sea?

7. Which city were both Katrina and The Waves and The Bangles going down to?

8. Which country was formerly known as East Pakistan?

9. Which Irish jockey recorded a hat-trick of wins in the Prix de L'Arc de Triomphe from 1985 to 1987?

10. Who was the second US President after George Washington?

11. An early example of what was called a 'Piggly Wiggly'?

12. What is an eddy?

13. What are the flowers of willows, poplars and birches called?

14. Which actor went from straight man to a puppet fox to a job as Private Secretary to the Prime Minister?

15. What is Gregory Peck's real Christian name?

16. Which two British athletes won long jump gold medals at the 1964 Tokyo Olympics?

Answers to page 58
QUIZ 57: **1.** Aston Villa **2.** Audrey Hepburn **3.** Irish **4.** Margarine **5.** Fe **6.** Switzerland **7.** Paul **8.** Tashkent **9.** Garbage **10.** Pike **11.** Chelmsford **12.** Holt **13.** Dale Winton (named after Dale Robertson) **14.** Tanzania **15.** Ian Baker-Finch **16.** Caspian Sea

Quiz 60

Answers on page 59

1. What is the colour of mourning in Turkey?

2. What three colours are on the flag of the Republic of Ireland?

3. How many countries border Belgium?

4. Who was the first presenter of *Grandstand*?

5. Which singer/actor was born Paul Beuselinck?

6. Which game takes its name from the Latin for a bird of prey?

7. The gourde is the currency of which country?

8. Whose companion was Captain Hastings?

9. Which eighties band took their name from two bowler-hatted secret service agents in *Hergé's Adventures of Tintin*?

10. Which star of *Gandhi* once chatted up Irma Barlow in *Coronation Street*?

11. In horse racing, what is the fillies' version of the Derby?

12. What was Shakespeare's last play?

13. Which actor suffered such bad stage fright during a production of *Cell Mates* that he left the country?

14. Foil, épee and sabre are the three types of weapon used in which sport?

15. What kind of musical instrument is a fife?

16. What nationality was the physician Galen?

Answers to page 59
QUIZ 58: **1.** Glenn Hoddle (after Glenn Miller) **2.** *Sabrina the Teenage Witch* **3.** African violet **4.** Accordion **5.** Kevin Costner **6.** Cambodia **7.** Guyana **8.** 1605 **9.** Heinrich Himmler **10.** Yorkshire **11.** Eucalyptus **12.** Gwynedd **13.** Boise **14.** Plastic Bertrand **15.** A club foot **16.** Vic Reeves

Quiz 61

Answers on page 64

1. Which son of a Yorkshire Test cricketer made his England debut in 2001?

2. 'Someday My Prince Will Come' is a song from which Disney film?

3. Which radio show celebrated its 50th birthday on 1 January 2001?

4. What was King Arthur's legendary seat?

5. What unit of work and energy has replaced the calorie?

6. What is the common name for convolvulus?

7. In which county is Silverstone motor-racing circuit?

8. Meg Richardson ran which TV establishment?

9. With which musical instrument was John William Coltrane associated?

10. Which of the Seven Wonders of the World fell victim to an earthquake in 224 BC?

11. Who starred in *Beau Geste* and *The Prisoner of Zenda*?

12. Which French philosopher said: 'I think, therefore I am'?

13. Which 1965 ballad was covered by 1,186 different performers in the first ten years?

14. Which is the largest moon in the solar system?

15. What is the capital of Bermuda?

16. Who played the drunken baseball coach in the 1992 movie *A League of their Own*?

Answers to page 64
QUIZ 63: **1.** Norvell **2.** Bob Geldof **3.** Basketball **4.** Concertina **5.** Zloty **6.** Renault **7.** Roman Polanski **8.** Coldplay **9.** The Oval **10.** Owls **11.** Cornwall **12.** Glenn Miller **13.** Nell Gwynn **14.** Benny Goodman **15.** Anne Frank **16.** Iris

Quiz 62

Answers on page 65

1. On which river does Hanoi stand?

2. Who cut off the tails of the Three Blind Mice?

3. Which rugby team won the Heineken Cup in 2000–1?

4. Which singer starred in *Memphis Belle*?

5. In Greek mythology, who was the daughter of Zeus and Leda?

6. What nationality was Henry the Navigator?

7. With what branch of music is John Lee Hooker associated?

8. Which English town has a tall church tower called a 'stump'?

9. Who was captain of Australia's cricket team from 1985 to 1994?

10. Who was the subject of the film *That Hamilton Woman* – Emma Hamilton or Christine Hamilton?

11. Who does Amanda Burton play in *Silent Witness*?

12. Which Jesse founded a pharmacy chain?

13. Which English river has a bore?

14. Which jockey, who rode 21 classic winners, shot himself in a fit of depression in 1886?

15. For what was Anzac an acronym?

16. Which is the most northerly of the major Greek islands?

Answers to page 65
QUIZ 64: **1.** Epsom (salts) **2.** *Cocktail* **3.** Cycling **4.** Blur **5.** Greg Dyke **6.** Frozen food **7.** Blue Ridge Mountains **8.** Czech Republic **9.** Freshwater fish **10.** Southampton **11.** American **12.** *Heathers* **13.** Kingcup **14.** Gary Lineker **15.** Lammas **16.** Illinois

Quiz 63

Answers on page 62

1. What was Oliver Hardy's real Christian name?

2. Whose first album for almost a decade was the 2001 release *Sex, Age and Death*?

3. What sport do the Harlem Globetrotters play?

4. Which musical instrument was invented by Charles Wheatstone?

5. What is the national currency of Poland?

6. Which motor manufacturing company was founded by the brothers Louis, Fernand and Marcel?

7. Who directed *Rosemary's Baby* and *Bitter Moon*?

8. Which band released the album *A Rush of Blood to the Head* in 2002?

9. Which ground was the venue for the Test match between England and Australia in 1880?

10. What can be barn, snowy or tawny?

11. In which county is the fishing port of Newlyn?

12. Who disappeared on a flight between England and France in 1944?

13. Who was the most famous orange-seller at London's Drury Lane Theatre?

14. Who was known as the 'King of Swing'?

15. Whose diary was finally published in full in 1989?

16. Which flower is also called a flag?

Answers to page 62
QUIZ 61: **1.** Ryan Sidebottom (son of Arnie) **2.** *Snow White* **3.** *The Archers* **4.** Camelot **5.** Joule
6. Bindweed **7.** Northamptonshire **8.** Crossroads Motel **9.** Saxophone **10.** Colossus of Rhodes
11. Ronald Colman **12.** René Descartes **13.** 'Yesterday' **14.** Ganymede **15.** Hamilton **16.** Tom Hanks

Quiz 64

Answers on page 63

1. What Surrey town gives its name to the common form of hydrated magnesium sulphate?

2. In which film did Tom Cruise play a slick bartender?

3. Chris Boardman won an Olympic gold medal in 1992 at which sport?

4. Dave Rowntree is the drummer with which band?

5. Who succeeded John Birt as director-general of the BBC?

6. What did Clarence Birdseye pioneer?

7. Which mountains extend from West Virginia to Georgia and were immortalised in a Laurel and Hardy song?

8. Bohemia is an area of which country?

9. What is a bleak?

10. Stuart Gray managed which Premiership football club at the start of season 2001–2?

11. What nationality was the painter Thomas Eakins?

12. Which 1989 movie starred Christian Slater and Winona Ryder as a pair of teenage murderers?

13. What is another name for the marsh marigold?

14. Which footballer moved to Japan in 1993 to play for Nagoya Grampus Eight?

15. Which harvest festival is celebrated on 1 August?

16. Which US state is nicknamed the 'Land of Lincoln'?

Answers to page 63
QUIZ 62: **1.** Red River **2.** The farmer's wife **3.** Leicester Tigers **4.** Harry Connick Jnr **5.** Helen
6. Portuguese **7.** Blues **8.** Boston **9.** Allan Border **10.** Emma Hamilton **11.** Sam Ryan **12.** Jesse Boot
13. Severn **14.** Fred Archer **15.** Australian and New Zealand Army Corps **16.** Corfu

Quiz 65

Answers on page 68

1. Which long-serving tennis commentator died in 1992?

2. If you were to spell out numbers (omitting the 'and'), what number would you have to go to before finding the letter 'a'?

3. In which country was Chris De Burgh born?

4. The anagram of which actress's name is 'evil lass in erotica'?

5. What pseudonym is used by author David Cornwell?

6. What is the name for an alloy of copper and tin?

7. Who founded Habitat?

8. What colours are the numbers on a roulette wheel?

9. In which English county is Althorp House?

10. Which comedian sold his wedding photos to *Viz* magazine for £1?

11. Who was sent off as England's footballers went out of the 1998 World Cup?

12. Donald McGill created 12,000 examples of what type of artwork?

13. Which band are led by Ian Broudie?

14. What does the *Venus de Milo* lack?

15. How many chambers are there in the human heart?

16. How many Football League teams are there in Kent?

Answers to page 68
QUIZ 67: **1.** Liverpool **2.** Pluto **3.** A phase of the Moon **4.** Antarctica **5.** Mike Rutherford
6. Viv Anderson **7.** Pingwings **8.** Walt Disney **9.** Spain **10.** Fear of the left side **11.** New Hampshire
12. Dolphin **13.** A backbone **14.** Roberts **15.** July **16.** Partition between the nostrils

Quiz 66

Answers on page 69

1. How many hearts does an earthworm have?

2. Which superstar sang backing vocals on Rockwell's 'Somebody's Watching You'?

3. Which *Blue Peter* presenter played one of Doctor Who's assistants?

4. A crop of which fruit dropped from the sky on to a Louisiana building-site in 1961?

5. The Flathead Lake Monster is said to exist in which American state?

6. Which racehorse named after a Russian dancer won the Two Thousand Guineas, Derby and St Leger in 1970?

7. Which swashbuckling trio were created by Alexandre Dumas?

8. Who played Crêpe Suzette in the film *Absolute Beginners*?

9. Durrës is the chief port of which country?

10. Which battle on British soil took place on 9 September 1513?

11. Who was the original presenter of the TV talent show *New Faces*?

12. What speed can a dragonfly reach?

13. What is unique about the Book of Esther in the Bible?

14. Which Thursday precipitated the worldwide Depression in 1929?

15. Who duetted with Peter Gabriel on 'Don't Give Up'?

16. Who composed the ballet *Swan Lake*?

Answers to page 69
QUIZ 68: **1.** Brian Clough **2.** Cumbria and Northumberland **3.** Van Morrison **4.** Tom and Jerry **5.** Donald Duck **6.** *Tess of the D'Urbervilles* **7.** Dorset **8.** North **9.** Motor-cycle racing **10.** London and Paris **11.** Miss Scarlett **12.** West Indies **13.** Trappist **14.** Lemon and melon **15.** Racehorses **16.** China

Quiz 67

Answers on page 66

1. Which is farthest west – Bristol, Liverpool or Cheltenham?

2. Which is the smallest planet?

3. What does the term gibbous describe?

4. Where is Queen Maud Land?

5. Who is the 'Mike' of Mike and the Mechanics?

6. Who was the first black player to appear for England in a full international?

7. Who lived on Berrydown Farm?

8. Although he had one himself, which movie studio boss refused to allow any of his employees to grow a moustache?

9. Which country hosts an annual mass tomato fight?

10. What is levophobia?

11. Which American state is nicknamed the 'Granite State'?

12. What kind of creature was Flipper?

13. What does an invertebrate lack?

14. What was Margaret Thatcher's maiden name?

15. In which month of the year is the British Open golf tournament held?

16. What is a septum?

Answers to page 66
QUIZ 65: **1.** Dan Maskell **2.** One thousand **3.** Argentina **4.** Alicia Silverstone **5.** John Le Carré **6.** Bronze **7.** Terence Conran **8.** Red and black **9.** Northamptonshire **10.** Johnny Vegas **11.** David Beckham **12.** Saucy seaside postcards **13.** The Lightning Seeds **14.** Arms **15.** Four **16.** One (Gillingham)

Quiz 68

Answers on page 67

1. Which football manager retired after leading Nottingham Forest to relegation in 1993?

2. Which two English counties border Scotland?

3. Which veteran Irish rock star used to be one of Them?

4. Which animated protagonists were condemned in the 1970s for their 'mindless violence'?

5. Who was translated as Donald Anus by the Vatican newspaper?

6. Angel Clare appeared in which Thomas Hardy novel?

7. Blandford Forum is in which county?

8. On which coast of France is Deauville?

9. In which sport do competitors go earholing?

10. Which are the two cities in *A Tale of Two Cities*?

11. Which Cluedo suspect is known as Fröken Röd in Scandinavia?

12. Leary Constantine played Test cricket for which country?

13. Which order of monks maintain a vow of silence?

14. Which two fruits are anagrams of each other?

15. What does Sir Michael Stoute train?

16. In which country were the Triads founded?

Answers to page 67
QUIZ 66: **1.** Ten **2.** Michael Jackson **3.** Peter Purves **4.** Peaches **5.** Montana **6.** Nijinsky **7.** The Three Musketeers **8.** Patsy Kensit **9.** Albania **10.** Battle of Flodden **11.** Derek Hobson **12.** 25mph **13.** It is the only book of the Bible that doesn't mention God by name **14.** Black Thursday **15.** Kate Bush **16.** Tchaikovsky

Quiz 69

Answers on page 72

1. Who was the first driver to win the Formula One World Championship in his own make of car?

2. At which Irish battle in 1690 was James II defeated by William III?

3. On a compass, which point is directly opposite south-south-west?

4. What is the main prey of the monkey-eating eagle?

5. The Tyrrehenian Sea is situated to the west of which country?

6. What Oscar Wilde character possessed a supernatural picture?

7. Who survived 24 years of the old *Crossroads*, but was killed off three months after the return of the new series?

8. Relating to the time of day, what does p.m. stand for?

9. What is the capital of Tasmania?

10. Eddie Butler and Nigel Starmer-Smith are TV commentators on which sport?

11. Which country resigned from the Commonwealth in 1949?

12. Which entertainer was born Priscilla White?

13. Who became leader of the Labour Party in 1992?

14. When does an ounce have four legs?

15. In what type of bowling did West Indies cricketer Lance Gibbs specialise?

16. Which American Indian chief was killed at Wounded Knee?

Answers to page 72
QUIZ 71: **1.** Rome **2.** Vegetable **3.** Spain **4.** Hong Kong **5.** Montague and Capulet **6.** The eye
7. Zsa Zsa Gabor **8.** *The Dukes of Hazzard* **9.** Electrical voltage **10.** Its hot springs **11.** The heel
12. Pepsi-Cola **13.** Lanfranco **14.** 'Rotterdam' **15.** Belgian **16.** Norman Mailer

Quiz 70

Answers on page 73

1. Andorra lies between which two countries?

2. What did the Knave of Hearts steal?

3. Formentera is part of which group of islands?

4. As what did Sir John Barbirolli make his name?

5. Which author's real name was Charles Lutwidge Dodgson?

6. Which Michael Cimino film starring Robert De Niro won the Oscar for Best Picture in 1978?

7. Which Great Dane joined Aston Villa in 2001?

8. Who presents *Big Brother*?

9. The entire population of which country were sentenced to death in their absence by the Spanish Inquisition?

10. What is the name for a female swan?

11. Of which Prime Minister did Malcolm Muggeridge once say: 'He is not only a bore, but he bores for England'?

12. Who was non-playing captain of Europe's triumphant 1985 Ryder Cup golf team?

13. Which 150–1 outsider became World Snooker Champion in 1986?

14. Under which name did Sister Luc-Gabrielle have a surprise 1963 hit?

15. In which century did brown bears become extinct in the UK?

16. Which Victorian murderer was known as 'The Staffordshire Poisoner'?

Answers to page 73
QUIZ 72: **1.** 36 **2.** Semaphore **3.** Chicken **4.** Devon, Avon, Dorset and Wiltshire **5.** A wading bird **6.** Cairngorms **7.** Colonel Harry Llewellyn **8.** Louisa May Alcott **9.** *Gipsy Moth IV* **10.** Corky **11.** Mud **12.** Sweeney Todd **13.** It was contested by two English teams – Bristol City and Tranmere Rovers **14.** Corona **15.** Wilpur Post **16.** On a trampoline

Quiz 71

Answers on page 70

1. Lazio Football Club play their home games in which city?

2. What is a mangelwurzel?

3. Navarre is a mountain region of which country?

4. In which harbour did the *Queen Elizabeth* liner sink in 1972?

5. What were the names of the opposing families in *Romeo and Juliet*?

6. What does an ophthalmologist study?

7. Who said: 'I never hated a man enough to give him his diamonds back'?

8. Luke, Bo and Daisy were cousins in which TV series?

9. What does an oscilloscope measure?

10. What is the New Zealand town of Rotorua renowned for?

11. Where is the human skin least sensitive?

12. What was the first US consumer product to be sold in the Soviet Union?

13. What is jockey Frankie Dettori's full Christian name?

14. Which Dutch port provided The Beautiful South with a 1996 hit?

15. What nationality was the artist Magritte?

16. Which American novelist wrote *The Executioner's Song*?

Answers to page 70
QUIZ 69: **1.** Jack Brabham **2.** Battle of the Boyne **3.** North-north-east **4.** Flying lemurs **5.** Italy **6.** Dorian Gray **7.** Jill Richardson/Harvey Chance **8.** Post meridiem **9.** Hobart **10.** Rugby union **11.** Republic of Ireland **12.** Cilla Black **13.** John Smith **14.** When it's another name for a snow leopard **15.** Off-spin **16.** Sitting Bull

Quiz 72

Answers on page 71

1. What do the numbers go up to on a roulette wheel?

2. What is the name for the visual signalling code conducted with flags?

3. If you ordered 'pollo' in an Italian restaurant, what would you be served?

4. Which four counties border Somerset?

5. What is an avocet?

6. In which mountain range is the town of Aviemore?

7. Who rode a clear round on Foxhunter to give Britain an equestrian gold medal at the 1952 Olympics?

8. Who wrote *Little Women*?

9. In which yacht did Sir Francis Chichester sail solo around the world?

10. What was the name of the friendly neighbourhood policeman in *Sykes*?

11. Which band were feeling 'Lonely This Christmas' in 1974?

12. Who was the demon barber of Fleet Street?

13. In football, what was unusual about the 1934 Welsh Cup final?

14. What is the name for the outermost part of the Sun's atmosphere?

15. Who owned the talking horse Mister Ed?

16. Where are adolphs, randolphs and rudolphs performed?

Answers to page 71
QUIZ 70: **1.** France and Spain **2.** Tarts **3.** Balearic **4.** Conductor **5.** Lewis Carroll **6.** *The Deer Hunter* **7.** Peter Schmeichel **8.** Davina McCall **9.** The Netherlands **10.** Pen **11.** Anthony Eden **12.** Tony Jacklin **13.** Joe Johnson **14.** The Singing Nun **15.** 11th **16.** William Palmer

Quiz 73

Answers on page 76

1. What is an oryx?

2. Which composition by Ravel was performed on ice by Torvill and Dean?

3. As whom was Grigory Efimovich better known in early 20th-century Russia?

4. Which TV soap is set in Charnham?

5. Which band released the seventies albums *A Question Of Balance*, *Every Good Boy Deserves Favour* and *Seventh Sojourn*?

6. Which film studios in west London were renowned for their post-war comedies, often starring Alec Guinness?

7. On which racecourse is the St Leger run?

8. What unit is used to measure the fineness of yarns, as in nylon stockings?

9. Which English king was known as 'the Unready'?

10. Which star of *Red River* and *From Here to Eternity* was disfigured in a car crash in 1957?

11. Which 14-year-old Romanian gymnast won three gold medals at the 1976 Montreal Olympics?

12. Which former British Prime Minister died on 29 December 1986?

13. The theme from which TV series gave Nick Berry a number two hit in 1992?

14. Which actress won the Miss Italy title in 1946?

15. Which brothers played for Australia's victorious cricketers against England in the summer of 2001?

16. Which American state is nicknamed 'the Sooner State'?

Answers to page 76
QUIZ 75: **1.** Neil Morrissey (the voice of Bob the Builder played Texas Ranger Rocky in the TV series *Boon*) **2.** Eddie Kelly (for Arsenal in 1971) **3.** Six – Belgium, Luxembourg, Germany, Switzerland, Italy and Spain **4.** *Home and Away* **5.** Wye **6.** Norgay **7.** Jeff Goldblum **8.** Patricia Highsmith **9.** Jasper Carrott **10.** Dolls **11.** Lyndon B. Johnson **12.** Gary Player **13.** California **14.** Dire Straits **15.** Mama Cass Elliott and Keith Moon **16.** Vincent Price

Quiz 74

Answers on page 77

1. What word featured in both of Art Garfunkel's solo number ones?

2. Which continent does the fierce snake come from?

3. Which actor, born Michael Dumble-Smith, took his stage name from a passing biscuit lorry?

4. Which antiseptic takes its name from trichlorophenol?

5. Which board game was invented by solicitor's clerk Anthony E. Pratt?

6. Which artist appeared in a crowd scene in Jean Cocteau's 1962 film *The Testament of Orpheus*?

7. Which was the 50th state to join the United States?

8. What was the name of the cow in *The Woodentops*?

9. Brian Horton managed which Football League club at the start of season 2001–2?

10. What is another name for the clavicle?

11. The gharial is a species of which reptile?

12. In which country is Krakow?

13. What is the largest island in the Caribbean?

14. What is the second book in the Old Testament?

15. What is the name for a plant which completes its life cycle in two years?

16. What was first erected in 1961?

Answers to page 77
QUIZ 76: **1.** The Outlaws **2.** Belgium **3.** 17 March **4.** Trafalgar **5.** Gardener/botanist **6.** Bruce Willis **7.** Captain and Tennille **8.** Suffragette Emily Davison died after throwing herself in front of the king's horse **9.** Maureen Connolly **10.** Lynmouth **11.** Bakelite **12.** Louis Blériot **13.** Dorset **14.** A bird **15.** Sir Galahad **16.** Four

Quiz 75

Answers on page 74

1. Who links Bob the Builder with The Texas Rangers?

2. Who was the first substitute to score in an FA Cup Final?

3. How many countries border France?

4. Which Australian soap returned to Britain on Channel 5 in 2001?

5. On which river does High Wycombe stand?

6. What was Sherpa Tenzing's surname?

7. Who starred in *The Tall Guy* and *Jurassic Park*?

8. Which Patricia wrote *The Talented Mr Ripley*?

9. Which comedian's 1975 single 'The Magic Roundabout' was banned by the BBC over its sexual content?

10. Pediophobia is a fear of what?

11. Which American President had a wife named Ladybird?

12. Which veteran golfer is known as 'the man in black'?

13. Pasadena is a city in which American state?

14. Which band's best-selling album of the 1980s was titled *Brothers In Arms*?

15. Which two rock stars died separately in the same London apartment owned by Harry Nilsson?

16. Which horror movie actor co-starred with Elvis Presley in *The Trouble With Girls*?

Answers to page 74
QUIZ 73: **1.** A large antelope **2.** *Boléro* **3.** Rasputin **4.** *Family Affairs* **5.** The Moody Blues **6.** Ealing
7. Doncaster **8.** Denier **9.** Ethelred **10.** Montgomery Clift **11.** Nadia Comaneci **12.** Harold Macmillan
13. *Heartbeat* **14.** Gina Lollobrigida **15.** Steve and Mark Waugh **16.** Oklahoma

Quiz 76

Answers on page 75

1. What is the nickname of Nottinghamshire's Norwich Union League cricket team?

2. In which country is Passchendaele?

3. What date is St Patrick's Day?

4. At which battle was Admiral Nelson mortally wounded?

5. In which field did John Tradescant make his name?

6. Who shaved his head for the film *Twelve Monkeys*?

7. Which married couple had a hit with 'Do That To Me One More Time'?

8. What incident marred the 1913 Epsom Derby?

9. Which tennis player was known as 'Little Mo'?

10. Which North Devon town was devastated by a freak flood in August 1952?

11. Which commercial plastic was invented by Leo Baekeland?

12. Who made the first flight across the English Channel?

13. In which county is Corfe Castle?

14. What is a chough?

15. In Arthurian legend, who was the son of Sir Lancelot?

16. How many stomachs does a cow have?

Answers to page 75
QUIZ 74: **1.** 'Eyes' ('I Only Have Eyes For You' and 'Bright Eyes') **2.** Australia **3.** Michael Crawford **4.** TCP **5.** Cluedo **6.** Pablo Picasso **7.** Hawaii **8.** Buttercup **9.** Port Vale **10.** Collar bone **11.** Crocodile **12.** Poland **13.** Cuba **14.** Exodus **15.** Biennial **16.** The Berlin Wall

Quiz 77

Answers on page 80

1. Who searched for the one-armed man in *The Fugitive*?

2. Mike Barson was the chief songwriter with which eighties band?

3. What does EMU stand for?

4. What is a smolt?

5. What is the Japanese wine saké made from?

6. Which Fulke was a well-known racehorse trainer?

7. What was the name of *Perry Mason*'s secretary?

8. Which group backed Johnny Kidd?

9. What was St Vitus the patron saint of?

10. The London Promenade Concerts are named after which conductor?

11. For which film did Emma Thompson win an Oscar for Best Actress in 1992?

12. Which Formula One Grand Prix takes place at Interlagos?

13. A bombardon is a member of which group of musical instruments?

14. What was the first name of the German dramatist Brecht?

15. Who was the youngest of the three Brontë sisters?

16. Who wrote *Hotel du Lac*?

Answers to page 80
QUIZ 79: **1.** Johnny Nash **2.** Willie Johnston **3.** Italy **4.** Queen Anne **5.** 23 Railway Cuttings, East Cheam **6.** Denmark **7.** Apollo XI **8.** Pierce **9.** Ruby Murray **10.** *Play Misty For Me* **11.** Mick Jagger **12.** South America **13.** Fulham Broadway **14.** Marylebone **15.** Japan **16.** Crossword puzzle

Quiz 78

Answers on page 81

1. Which hero of spaghetti Westerns is allergic to horses?

2. What did Arsenal and Chelsea have on 25 August 1928 that no other team did?

3. Who was the first woman in space?

4. What were the young men of Britain no longer required to perform after 1960?

5. Whose 1995 album was *Different Class*?

6. In which Irish county is Connemara?

7. Who announced that he was going to leave old Durham town?

8. Who composed the 'Brandenburg Concertos'?

9. What animal lives in a sett?

10. To what family of birds does the blackcap belong?

11. What were followers of Oswald Mosley's British Union of Fascists commonly known as?

12. Which romantic novelist's first book was *Jigsaw*, published in 1921?

13. In which Dublin park were two prominent members of the British government murdered in 1882?

14. Who was Starsky and Hutch's jive-talking informant?

15. Who invented the Polaroid camera?

16. In which US state does the Rio Grande river rise?

Answers to page 81
QUIZ 80: **1.** 6th century BC **2.** Dissolvable aspirin **3.** Mr Black **4.** Botswana **5.** Bangkok **6.** Chickens **7.** Incontinence **8.** Mexico **9.** Those fascinated by handwriting **10.** Longstreet **11.** Northampton Town **12.** Pregnant **13.** Anita Dobson **14.** Denis Healey **15.** Michael Palin **16.** Algeria

Quiz 79

Answers on page 78

1. Whose only UK number one single was 'Tears on my Pillow'?

2. Which Scottish international footballer was sent home in disgrace from the 1978 World Cup finals after testing positive for drugs that were contained in a cold remedy?

3. In which country is the resort of Rimini?

4. Who was the last Stuart sovereign of England?

5. Where did Tony Hancock live in *Hancock's Half Hour*?

6. Which country rules the Faeroe Islands?

7. Which American space mission took Neil Armstrong and Buzz Aldrin to the Moon?

8. What was the surname of 'Hawkeye' in *M*A*S*H*?

9. Who had five hits in the Top Twenty at the same time in 1955?

10. On which film did Clint Eastwood make his debut as a director?

11. Which Rolling Stone once worked as a porter at a mental hospital?

12. From which continent does the potato originate?

13. Which London Underground station was called Walham Green until 1952?

14. Which London railway terminus is at the end of the Chiltern Line?

15. Which country uses more condoms than any other?

16. What pastime did Arthur Wynne invent in 1913?

Answers to page 78
QUIZ 77: **1.** Dr Richard Kimble **2.** Madness **3.** European Monetary Union **4.** A young salmon **5.** Rice **6.** Fulke Walwyn **7.** Della Street **8.** The Pirates **9.** Dancers **10.** Henry Wood **11.** *Howard's End* **12.** Brazilian **13.** Brass **14.** Bertolt **15.** Anne **16.** Anita Brookner

Quiz 80

Answers on page 79

1. In which century did the first known dictionary appear?

2. What is Disprin short for?

3. Who is the perpetual victim in Cluedo?

4. Which country used to be known as Bechuanaland?

5. Which Oriental capital city means 'wild plum village'?

6. Alektorophobia is a fear of what?

7. According to medieval beliefs, what was urinating on an open grave supposed to cure?

8. In which country do they celebrate the Day of the Dead on 2 November?

9. For what does the Cheirological Society cater?

10. Who was TV's first blind detective?

11. Which Football League team are nicknamed the 'Cobblers'?

12. What perfectly natural word was Lucille Ball banned from saying in *I Love Lucy*?

13. Which future landlady of the Queen Vic appeared on *Play Away*?

14. Who was the only human to appear on *Spitting Image*?

15. Which member of the *Monty Python* team once appeared as a surfer on *Home and Away*?

16. Which country achieved independence from France in 1962?

Answers to page 79
QUIZ 78: **1.** Clint Eastwood **2.** Numbered shirts **3.** Valentina Tereshkova **4.** National service **5.** Pulp **6.** Galway **7.** Roger Whittaker **8.** Bach **9.** Badger **10.** Warbler **11.** Blackshirts **12.** Dame Barbara Cartland **13.** Phoenix Park **14.** Huggy Bear **15.** Dr Edwin Land **16.** South Colorado

Quiz 81

Answers on page 84

1. In cookery what is cayenne?

2. In which American state is the town of Cedar Rapids?

3. Which English king's lover was Piers Gaveston?

4. What is an epigram?

5. Which 1998 film about a shy girl who can sing like her showbiz idols starred Jane Horrocks and Michael Caine?

6. At which sport do England and Scotland compete for the Calcutta Cup?

7. Which is the world's oldest football knockout competition?

8. In which year did Abba reach number one in the UK with 'Knowing Me, Knowing You'?

9. Where in the world has the busiest roads?

10. Which country lies immediately to the south of Belarus?

11. Which TV magician gave Basil Brush his big break?

12. Which Argentinian cruiser was controversially sunk by British forces during the Falklands conflict with the loss of nearly 400 men?

13. In May 1982, what happened in Britain for the first time for 450 years?

14. Which former dress-wearing member of Mud has co-written number one hits for Spiller and Kylie Minogue?

15. Which bird is noted for its boom?

16. In France, what would you buy from a boulangerie?

Answers to page 84

QUIZ 83: **1.** Bob Hoskins **2.** *The Forsyte Saga* **3.** 1988 **4.** Panama Canal **5.** Portuguese **6.** 'The Divine Comedy' **7.** Melchester Rovers **8.** John Reginald Christie **9.** St Bernard **10.** The Faeroe Islands **11.** North America **12.** Sardinia **13.** Arsenal **14.** Field hockey **15.** Milkman **16.** Sharon Watts

Quiz 82

Answers on page 85

1. Whose short story *The Birds* was made into a Hitchcock thriller?

2. Which Shakespeare play begins: 'Now is the winter of our discontent'?

3. What is a horsetail?

4. In the Old Testament, which daughter of the King of Sidon married King Ahab of Israel?

5. Which boy band had the first new UK number one single of the 1990s?

6. Zealand, Fyn, Lolland, Falster and Bornholm are the principal islands of which country?

7. Which American city was hit by an earthquake in 1994, killing 61 people?

8. Who starred with Tom Cruise in the 1983 comedy *Risky Business*?

9. On a golf course, what is the name of the close-cut grass around the edge of the green?

10. Which decade in the USA is commonly referred to as the Jazz Age?

11. Which popular grey horse won the Cheltenham Gold Cup in 1989?

12. What is the term for the sensation that something encountered for the first time has actually been seen before?

13. Which boxer succeeded Henry Cooper as British heavyweight champion?

14. What three colours appear on the flag of Bulgaria?

15. Which country has the busiest rail network in the world?

16. What did Lovejoy deal in?

Answers to page 85
QUIZ 84: **1.** Portugal **2.** September **3.** Jamaica **4.** Vinnie Jones **5.** Cheshire **6.** Birdwatcher **7.** Helen Baxendale **8.** Brugge **9.** Alberta **10.** Citroën **11.** Guy Fawkes **12.** Rhythmic gymnastics **13.** Two **14.** Edinburgh **15.** Herbert Asquith **16.** George Michael

Quiz 83

Answers on page 82

1. Who played London crime lord Harold Shand in *The Long Good Friday*?

2. *The Man of Property* was the first part of which series of novels?

3. In which year did Bros reach number one with 'I Owe You Nothing'?

4. Where is the only place in the world that you can see the sun rise over the Pacific and set over the Atlantic?

5. Estoril is the venue of which Formula One Grand Prix?

6. Neil Hannon took his band name from which epic poem by Dante Alighieri?

7. For which football club did Roy Race play for many years?

8. Who committed the murders on which the film *10 Rillington Place* was based?

9. What breed of dog was Beethoven in the film of the same name?

10. Which country's national dish is puffin stuffed with rhubarb?

11. The Porcupine River is in which continent?

12. On which island is the town of Cagliari?

13. Who did Liverpool defeat in the 2001 FA Cup Final?

14. Which game starts with a bully?

15. What was Ernie's occupation in the Benny Hill number one hit?

16. Who returned to *EastEnders* as co-owner of the Queen Vic in 2001?

Answers to page 82
QUIZ 81: **1.** Pepper **2.** Iowa **3.** Edward II **4.** A short, witty saying **5.** *Little Voice* **6.** Rugby union **7.** FA Cup **8.** 1977 **9.** Hong Kong **10.** Ukraine **11.** David Nixon **12.** *General Belgrano* **13.** The Pope visited Britain **14.** Rob Davis **15.** Bittern **16.** Bread

Quiz 84

Answers on page 83

1. Coimbra and Setubal are towns in which European country?

2. In which month of the year is the St Leger run?

3. Kingston is the capital of which island?

4. Which former footballer played Big Chris in *Lock, Stock and Two Smoking Barrels*?

5. In which English county is Crewe?

6. What is a twitcher?

7. Who played Rachel in *Cold Feet*?

8. What is the Flemish name for Bruges?

9. In which Canadian province is Calgary?

10. Which French motor company was bought by Peugeot in 1974?

11. Who was arrested in the cellar beneath the Houses of Parliament on 4 November 1605?

12. A ribbon, ball or hoop are accessories in which sporting floor exercise?

13. How many wheels does a hansom cab have?

14. Where is Arthur's Seat?

15. Who was British Prime Minister at the outbreak of the First World War?

16. Whose debut solo album was titled *Faith*?

Answers to page 83
QUIZ 82: **1.** Daphne du Maurier **2.** *Richard III* **3.** A plant **4.** Jezebel **5.** New Kids on the Block **6.** Denmark **7.** Los Angeles **8.** Rebecca De Mornay **9.** Apron **10.** 1920s **11.** Desert Orchid **12.** *Déjà vu* **13.** Joe Bugner **14.** White, green and red **15.** Japan **16.** Antiques

Quiz 85

Answers on page 88

1. What happened if suspects drowned during trial by ordeal?

2. What was Napoleon in a George Orwell novel?

3. What do actors Anthony Newley, James Booth, Terence Stamp and Laurence Harvey have in common?

4. Which band was formed in 1989 by Johnny Marr and Bernard Sumner?

5. Who was Benton Fraser's first partner in *Due South*?

6. What type of creature is a painted lady?

7. Which actor's first name means 'cool breeze over the mountains' in Hawaiian?

8. Who succeeded Ruud Gullit as manager of Chelsea?

9. Of whom did Irving Layton once say: 'At last Canada has produced a political leader worthy of assassination'?

10. Who was England's goalkeeper in the 1966 World Cup Final?

11. Who played Jinx in the Bond film *Die Another Day*?

12. Which British athlete set a women's world record at the 2002 Chicago Marathon?

13. Cirrhosis particularly attacks which organ of the body?

14. What can be electric or jellied?

15. May Hardman was the first death in which TV soap?

16. The lines of which army were drawn up by William Booth?

Answers to page 88
QUIZ 87: **1.** C.S. Forester **2.** Helsinki **3.** New Zealand **4.** Puff Daddy **5.** Ice skating **6.** Bill Grundy **7.** He was captain of the *Titanic* **8.** Red and white **9.** A US newspaper publisher **10.** Lambeth North **11.** Enzo Ferrari **12.** Brilliantine and cream **13.** Baghdad **14.** Rowley Birkin QC **15.** Equestrian three-day event **16.** Shropshire

Quiz 86

Answers on page 89

1. Who played a character ageing from 17 to 121 in *Little Big Man*?

2. What was the sequel to *Naked Gun 2½: The Smell of Fear*?

3. As whom was Francis Morgan Thompson better known?

4. With which band was Lionel Richie the lead singer before embarking on a solo career?

5. How many years are celebrated by a ruby anniversary?

6. Where in Britain would you find Robin Hood's Bay?

7. At what temperature Fahrenheit does water boil?

8. What does QC stand for?

9. Which planet was first located in 1846?

10. In *Great Expectations*, whose room had remained untouched for decades?

11. Maastricht is a town in which European country?

12. What shape is something that is falcate?

13. In what type of bowling does cricketer Shane Warne specialise?

14. What is the principal ingredient in a guacamole dip?

15. Which duck was guarded by Chopper the bulldog?

16. Which French couturier pioneered the mini skirt with Britain's Mary Quant?

Answers to page 89

QUIZ 88: **1.** *Some Like It Hot* **2.** Five **3.** Benny Hill **4.** Malmö **5.** World Snooker final **6.** The Mini **7.** Juggernaut **8.** Marie Antoinette **9.** Madge Bishop **10.** H.G. Wells **11.** The Alps **12.** Canada **13.** Lord Byron **14.** Malcolm and Donald Campbell **15.** P.D. James **16.** Electric guitar

Quiz 87

Answers on page 86

1. Who created Horatio Hornblower?

2. What is the capital of Finland?

3. In which country was the 1993 film *The Piano* set?

4. As whom did rapper Sean Combs find fame?

5. In which sport might you perform a double axel and a lutz?

6. Who said to The Sex Pistols: 'Go on, you've got another ten seconds. Say something outrageous'?

7. What was Captain Edward Smith's principal role in nautical history?

8. What two colours feature on the Swiss national flag?

9. Who was Gordon Bennett?

10. Which London Underground station was called Westminster Bridge Road until 1917?

11. Which Enzo founded one of the world's leading car manufacturers?

12. Brylcreem is an amalgamation of which two ingredients?

13. The name of which Middle East capital means 'God's gift'?

14. Who was invariably 'very, very drunk' on *The Fast Show*?

15. The dressage is part of which Olympic event?

16. Ironbridge is in which English county?

Answers to page 86
QUIZ 85: **1.** They were found innocent **2.** A pig **3.** They all turned down Michael Caine's role in *Alfie* **4.** Electronic **5.** Ray Vecchio **6.** Butterfly **7.** Keanu Reeves **8.** Gianluca Vialli **9.** Pierre Trudeau **10.** Gordon Banks **11.** Halle Berry **12.** Paula Radcliffe **13.** Liver **14.** Eels **15.** *Coronation Street* **16.** The Salvation Army

Quiz 88

Answers on page 87

1. In which 1959 film did Tony Curtis and Jack Lemmon appear in drag?

2. How many points is the letter 'K' worth in Scrabble?

3. Which comedian was born Alfred Hawthorne Hill?

4. Which is Sweden's most southerly city?

5. Which sporting event of 1985 attracted 18.6 million viewers in the early hours of the morning?

6. Which small car created a motoring revolution when it was introduced in 1959?

7. Which type of lorry is named after a Hindu god?

8. Who came out with the immortal line: 'Let them eat cake'?

9. Which *Neighbours* stalwart died in 2001?

10. Who wrote *The War of the Worlds*?

11. The Simplon tunnel runs beneath which range of mountains?

12. In which country is the Wood Buffalo national park?

13. Which English poet became a Greek national hero?

14. Which British father and son each held the world land and water speed records?

15. Who created the detective Adam Dalgliesh?

16. With which musical instrument is Duane Eddy associated?

Answers to page 87
QUIZ 86: **1.** Dustin Hoffman **2.** *Naked Gun 33¹/₃: The Final Insult* **3.** Daley Thompson
4. The Commodores **5.** 40 **6.** North Yorkshire **7.** 212 degrees **8.** Queen's Counsel **9.** Neptune
10. Miss Havisham **11.** The Netherlands **12.** Hooked **13.** Leg spin **14.** Avocado **15.** Yakky Doodle
16. André Courrèges

Quiz 89

Answers on page 92

1. What is receding from the Earth by an inch and a half per year?

2. What are wood mosaic and wood parquet?

3. In which Football League fixture would the Lions play the Tigers?

4. How many mountains in the world are over 28,000ft?

5. In which country is the Mojave Desert?

6. Which team currently playing in the Scottish First Division won the Scottish FA Cup in 1987?

7. Which racecourse hosts a July meeting that is always described as 'glorious'?

8. At what age did Robbie Williams join Take That?

9. What does the Russian word 'soyuz' mean, as in the series of spacecraft?

10. In which country is the port of Veracruz?

11. Who wrote *Cat on a Hot Tin Roof*?

12. On which island is Carisbrooke Castle?

13. Which English king was the illegitimate son of Duke Robert the Devil?

14. Who played the AIDS-stricken lawyer in the movie *Philadelphia*?

15. Which nationalist assumed the title 'governor of Scotland' in 1297?

16. Which *EastEnders* character is played by Charlie Brooks?

Answers to page 92
QUIZ 91: **1.** Jodie Foster **2.** Barings **3.** Jamie Oliver **4.** *Bob and Rose* **5.** Blarney Stone (Blarney Castle) **6.** Henry VI **7.** Michael Parkinson **8.** Japanese method of massage **9.** Putney **10.** Art **11.** Madonna **12.** Gold **13.** A plant **14.** Concrete **15.** Joseph Heller **16.** Wrestling

Quiz 90

Answers on page 93

1. In which city was the first Guggenheim Museum established?

2. Who wrote *Lord of the Flies*?

3. Which TV soap celebrated its 40th birthday in 2000?

4. Which French river has the same name as an evergreen US female singer?

5. Which is colder – minus 5 degrees Centigrade or minus 5 degrees Fahrenheit?

6. At sea, what do 6,080ft equal?

7. Which Russian woman won gold medals in the 800 and 1,500 metres at the 1996 Olympics?

8. In which English county is Tewkesbury?

9. In which century was golf first played?

10. Who was the Nazi minister of propaganda?

11. What are the factors of 8?

12. In which year was archery reintroduced to the Olympics?

13. Which state forms the northern border of North Carolina?

14. Which two brothers were members of Spandau Ballet?

15. Bob Hoskins played sheet music salesman Arthur Parker in which TV series by Dennis Potter?

16. In 1961, who beat Christine Truman in an all-British women's singles final at Wimbledon?

Answers to page 93
QUIZ 92: **1.** *Beau Geste* **2.** Ireland **3.** Uriah Heep **4.** Alfred Wainwright **5.** Ireland **6.** John Schlesinger **7.** 25 **8.** Vipers **9.** Turkey **10.** UNCLE **11.** Joe DiMaggio **12.** Terry Spinks and Dick McTaggart **13.** That a British expedition had become the first to conquer Everest **14.** The Milk Race **15.** Prague **16.** Harry Enfield and Paul Whitehouse

Quiz 91

Answers on page 90

1. Which star of *Little Man Tate* became a mother for the second time in October 2001?

2. For which bank did 'rogue trader' Nick Leeson work?

3. Which TV cook was embarrassed when a 12-year-old girl spat out his food in front of 3,000 people?

4. Which ITV series of 2001 was billed as a British version of the US sitcom *Will and Grace*?

5. What part of an Irish castle do visitors kiss for good luck?

6. Which English king was married to Margaret of Anjou?

7. Which TV chat show host celebrated the 30th anniversary of his programme in 2001?

8. What is shiatsu?

9. Where does the Boat Race start?

10. For what is the Turner Prize awarded?

11. Who has children named Lourdes and Rocco?

12. With what did Dick Whittington hope to find the streets of London paved?

13. What is shepherd's purse?

14. On what surface is the US Open tennis championship played?

15. Who wrote *Catch-22*?

16. Greco-Roman is a style of which sport?

Answers to page 90
QUIZ 89: **1.** The Moon **2.** Types of hardwood flooring **3.** Millwall v Hull **4.** Three **5.** USA
6. St Mirren **7.** Goodwood **8.** 16 **9.** 'Union' **10.** Mexico **11.** Tennessee Williams **12.** Isle of Wight
13. William the Conqueror **14.** Tom Hanks **15.** William Wallace **16.** Janine Butcher

Quiz 92

Answers on page 91

1. Which story of the Foreign Legion was written by P.C. Wren?

2. In which country was the Duke of Wellington born?

3. Which Dickens character was 'ever so 'umble'?

4. Which Alfred was an author of walkers' guidebooks?

5. In which country is there a rugby club called Garryowen?

6. Which Englishman directed *Midnight Cowboy*?

7. On a dart board, what is the value of the outer ring of the bull's-eye?

8. What can be horned, carpet or gaboon?

9. In which country is Lake Van?

10. Which organisation's headquarters were behind Del Floria's tailor shop in Manhattan?

11. Which baseball player featured in the lyrics of Simon and Garfunkel's 'Mrs Robinson'?

12. Which two British boxers won gold medals at the 1956 Olympics?

13. Which news reached London on the day of Elizabeth II's coronation?

14. What was the Tour of Britain cycling race previously known as?

15. Which European capital stands on the River Vltava?

16. Who played Smashey and Nicey?

Answers to page 91
QUIZ 90: **1.** New York **2.** William Golding **3.** *Coronation Street* **4.** Cher **5.** Fahrenheit **6.** One nautical mile **7.** Svetlana Masterkova **8.** Gloucestershire **9.** 15th **10.** Joseph Goebbels **11.** 1, 8, 2, 4 **12.** 1972 **13.** Virginia **14.** Gary and Martin Kemp **15.** *Pennies From Heaven* **16.** Angela Mortimer

Quiz 93

Answers on page 96

1. What is the Italian dish 'zuppa inglese'?

2. What type of animals did *ALF* most enjoy eating?

3. What colour is the leather on the seats in the House of Commons?

4. Which ship sank in the film *A Night to Remember*?

5. What action causes all your bodily functions to stop momentarily?

6. Which country produces the cheese Gaperon?

7. On this earth, what outnumber humans by approximately 100 million to one?

8. How long are baby kangaroos at birth?

9. What carnivores can smell humans up to 20 miles away?

10. Who released the best-selling UK album of 1999, *Come On Over*?

11. The Road Hole is part of which championship golf course?

12. *Jason King* was a spin-off from which TV series?

13. In which country is Eindhoven?

14. Which mountain in Alaska was named after a former US President?

15. What is London's Central Criminal Court more commonly known as?

16. How many lines are there in a sonnet?

Answers to page 96
QUIZ 95: **1.** The Andes **2.** Sebastian Coe **3.** Robert Maxwell **4.** Joy **5.** Marvin **6.** Mexico **7.** Pavement
8. Nine **9.** Winston Churchill **10.** The little dog **11.** Five **12.** Australia **13.** 'Angel of Harlem'
14. Cardiff **15.** Badger **16.** Great grey slug

Quiz 94

Answers on page 97

1. At which 2002 Grand Prix did Michael Schumacher secure his fifth Formula One World Drivers' Championship?

2. Which Poet Laureate wrote detective novels under the name Nicholas Blake?

3. What year followed 1 BC?

4. What is the national anthem of Australia?

5. Where is the Old Man of Coniston?

6. Which puppet is known in Germany is Balduin Schwupp?

7. Which British boxing hero from the 2000 Sydney Olympics turned professional shortly afterwards?

8. Flashman was the school bully in which novel?

9. Which footballer teamed up with Lindisfarne for a 1990 re-make of 'Fog on the Tyne'?

10. In which country is the Po River?

11. Which actress was known as 'America's Sweetheart'?

12. What is Monday's child said to be?

13. Which Hollywood dancer was born Eugene Curran?

14. Ratabaga is another name for which vegetable?

15. In which century was the Book of Kells produced?

16. The capital of which country switched from Alma-Ata to Astana in 1997?

Answers to page 97
QUIZ 96: **1.** Florida **2.** Giraffes **3.** Michelle Pfeiffer **4.** French **5.** Cordon bleu **6.** The Cure **7.** The Oaks **8.** Portugal **9.** Marlon Brando **10.** 1938 **11.** The Pony Express **12.** The Velvet Underground **13.** Gordon Strachan **14.** Skiffle **15.** Tobermory **16.** Regina

Quiz 95

Answers on page 94

1. What is the second highest mountain range in the world?

2. Which British athlete took silver in the 800 metres and gold in the 1,500 metres at both the 1980 and 1984 Olympics?

3. Who bought the *Mirror* newspaper group in 1984?

4. What are you supposed to feel if you see two magpies?

5. Who was the Paranoid Android in *The Hitch-Hiker's Guide to the Galaxy*?

6. Which country's national emblem depicts an eagle on a cactus devouring a snake?

7. What do Americans call a 'sidewalk'?

8. An ennead is a set of how many?

9. Which former Prime Minister wrote the four-volume *History of the English-Speaking Peoples*?

10. In the nursery rhyme 'Hey Diddle Diddle', which animal laughed to see such fun?

11. How many pillars of Islam are there?

12. In which continent is the Great Dividing Range of mountains?

13. Which U2 song was a tribute to singer Billie Holliday?

14. Which city lies at the mouth of the River Taff?

15. On children's TV, who was Simon Bodger's puppet pet?

16. Which creature mates in mid-air, hanging from a rope of slime?

Answers to page 94
QUIZ 93: **1.** Trifle **2.** Cats **3.** Green **4.** The *Titanic* **5.** Sneezing **6.** France **7.** Insects **8.** An inch **9.** Polar bears **10.** Shania Twain **11.** St Andrews **12.** *Department S* **13.** The Netherlands **14.** Mount McKinley **15.** Old Bailey **16.** 14

Quiz 96

Answers on page 95

1. In which American state are the Everglades?

2. Which are the only animals born with horns?

3. Who spread herself across a piano in *The Fabulous Baker Boys*?

4. What nationality was the artist Degas?

5. What name indicating cookery of a high standard is also given to a dish made with ham and cheese and a white sauce?

6. Which band had a 1983 hit with 'The Love Cats'?

7. Which was run first – the Derby or the Oaks?

8. Braganza was the royal house of which European country from 1640 to 1910?

9. Which actor's portrayal of biker Johnny in *The Wild One* created a rebel image?

10. In which year was the Munich Agreement?

11. What system of mail-carrying by relays of horse-riders was employed in parts of the USA in the 19th century?

12. Of which influential band was Lou Reed a member before going solo?

13. Which football club manager left Coventry City after just a few weeks of the 2001–2 season?

14. Which music style was pioneered by Lonnie Donegan?

15. Which Womble wore a black bowler hat?

16. What is the state capital of the Canadian province of Saskatchewan?

Answers to page 95
QUIZ 94: **1.** French **2.** Cecil Day-Lewis **3.** AD 1 **4.** 'Advance Australia Fair' **5.** In the Lake District **6.** Basil Brush **7.** Audley Harrison **8.** *Tom Brown's Schooldays* **9.** Paul Gascoigne **10.** Italy **11.** Mary Pickford **12.** Fair of face **13.** Gene Kelly **14.** Swede **15.** 8th **16.** Kazakhstan

Quiz 97

Answers on page 100

1. Who pioneered birth control in London in the 1920s?

2. What do Vanessa Feltz and Tony Curtis have in common?

3. Which singer had a Bionic Woman as babysitter for his children?

4. What is a stonechat?

5. In which county is Stilton cheese traditionally made?

6. Which cathedral has the tallest spire in England?

7. Which Russian city had three different names in the course of the 20th century?

8. What took place in Chicago on 14 February 1929?

9. With what instrument was jazz musician Sonny Rollins associated?

10. Soling, Finn and Tornado are categories in which sport?

11. Who sprinkled oofle dust?

12. As whom was Lev Davidovitch Bronstein better known?

13. When did Carole King decide it might as well rain until?

14. In which country is the fishing port of Trondheim?

15. Waverley Station is located in which British city?

16. What disease can the tsetse fly transmit to humans?

Answers to page 100
QUIZ 99: **1.** Lord Raglan **2.** Walker Cup **3.** *Me and My Girl* **4.** Lager **5.** Radius **6.** Poll tax **7.** 15th
8. Kate Winslet **9.** Pete Shelley was singer with The Buzzcocks and Mark Lamarr presents *Never Mind the Buzzcocks* **10.** Cross-Channel swim **11.** Coco Chanel **12.** Roald Dahl **13.** Richard Dadd
14. Australia **15.** Senegal **16.** Norfolk

Quiz 98

Answers on page 101

1. What did Barbie's boyfriend Ken originally lack which other boys had?

2. Which board game was devised by unemployed heating engineer Clarence B. Darrow?

3. What is the chemical term for chalk?

4. Which Benedictine monk invented champagne?

5. At which Olympic event did David Hemery win a gold medal?

6. What was Diana Prince's alter ego?

7. Which band's best-selling album was titled *Urban Hymns*?

8. Which writer of *The Hitch-Hiker's Guide to the Galaxy* died in 2001?

9. What is the name for a word that reads the same backwards as forwards?

10. What was the name of the lioness in *Born Free*?

11. In which English town is there a street called The Pantiles?

12. What do you call an angle which measures between 90 and 180 degrees?

13. In which forest was William II of England killed?

14. What did Wat Tyler lead in 1381?

15. On which river is Shrewsbury?

16. Who was banned from international football for a year in 1990 for insulting the French national team manager Henri Michel?

Answers to page 101
QUIZ 100: **1.** Olga Yegorova **2.** Samantha Failsworth **3.** 1,009 **4.** Lagos **5.** Oliver Stone **6.** Guinevere **7.** Scafell Pike **8.** *Chicago* **9.** Hamilton Academicals **10.** Britain **11.** Posture **12.** Browns, Seasons, Thickens-in-One **13.** Essex **14.** Kenneth Clark **15.** 1860s **16.** Dave Gilmour

Quiz 99

Answers on page 98

1. Which British field marshal in the Crimean War gave his name to a type of sleeve?

2. Which golf trophy did Britain and Ireland retain at Sea Island, Georgia, in August 2001?

3. Which musical features 'The Lambeth Walk'?

4. What sort of beer takes its name from the German for 'store'?

5. What is the name of the bone on the thumb side of the forearm?

6. What did the council tax replace in 1993?

7. In which century were the first reports of a Loch Ness monster?

8. Which actress split from husband Jim Threapleton in August 2001?

9. What links Pete Shelley and Mark Lamarr?

10. What was first achieved by Captain Matthew Webb in 1875?

11. Which fashion designer created the 'little black dress'?

12. Who wrote *Charlie and the Chocolate Factory*?

13. Which British painter murdered his father in 1843 and was committed to an asylum?

14. For which country did Neil Harvey play Test cricket?

15. Dakar is the capital of which African country?

16. In which county would you find the villages of Great Snoring and Little Snoring?

Answers to page 98
QUIZ 97: **1.** Marie Stopes **2.** Both have a daughter named Allegra **3.** Glen Campbell (Lindsay Wagner) **4.** A bird **5.** Leicestershire **6.** Salisbury **7.** St Petersburg – formerly Petrograd and Leningrad **8.** St Valentine's Day Massacre **9.** Tenor saxophone **10.** Yachting **11.** Sooty **12.** Trotsky **13.** September **14.** Norway **15.** Edinburgh **16.** Sleeping sickness

Quiz 100

Answers on page 99

1. Which Russian runner was booed as she won the women's 5,000 metres at the 2001 World Athletics Championships?

2. Which *Coronation Street* barmaid was played by Tina Hobley?

3. What is the lowest prime number over 1,000?

4. Which city was the capital of Nigeria until 1991?

5. Who directed *Platoon* and *JFK*?

6. In Arthurian legend, what was the name of King Arthur's wife?

7. What is the highest mountain in England?

8. Which musical won 13 Oscar nominations in 2003?

9. Which Scottish League football team were deducted 15 points in 2000 for refusing to fulfil a fixture at Stenhousemuir?

10. Albion was the ancient name for which country?

11. What is the Alexander technique said to improve?

12. What does Bisto stand for?

13. Where in Britain is Ugley?

14. Who popularised the history of art through the TV series *Civilisation*?

15. In which decade was the American Civil War?

16. Which member of Pink Floyd played guitar on Kate Bush's 'Wuthering Heights'?

Answers to page 99
QUIZ 98: **1.** Genitals **2.** Monopoly **3.** Calcium carbonate **4.** Dom Pérignon **5.** 400 metres hurdles **6.** *Wonder Woman* **7.** The Verve **8.** Douglas Adams **9.** Palindrome **10.** Elsa **11.** Tunbridge Wells **12.** Obtuse **13.** New Forest **14.** Peasants' Revolt **15.** Severn **16.** Eric Cantona

Quiz 101

Answers on page 104

1. What colours feature on the national flag of El Salvador?

2. What was introduced to Britain on 15 February 1971?

3. What did Norway's Johann Vaaler invent in 1900?

4. In which year did Shergar win the Derby?

5. The clarinet belongs to which group of musical instruments?

6. Which 17th-century judge conducted the 'bloody assizes'?

7. Brian Connolly was the singer with which seventies band?

8. What colour does jaundice make the skin?

9. The Battle of Inkerman took place during which war?

10. Who played Elizabeth R on TV?

11. What nationality was Henry the Navigator?

12. Who was Lenny the Lion's human partner?

13. Which is the only creature where the male becomes pregnant?

14. Which is the only domestic animal not mentioned in the Bible?

15. Which future Hollywood tough-guy had to wear his sister's hand-me-down dresses to school because his family were so poor?

16. Which Cherokee Indian had a UK number one hit in 1958?

Answers to page 104

QUIZ 103: **1.** Justin Henry **2.** Hungarian **3.** Nick Heidfeld **4.** Coniston Water **5.** Clint Eastwood **6.** Leonid Brezhnev **7.** Buzz Aldrin **8.** Duke of Buckingham **9.** Samuel Taylor Coleridge **10.** Marmalade **11.** Iceland (Eidur Gudjohnsen came on for father Arnor) **12.** Charles Edward Stuart **13.** Red deer **14.** Southern **15.** Hovis **16.** Northamptonshire

Quiz 102

Answers on page 105

1. Who became President of France following the resignation of Charles de Gaulle?

2. Which two artists had UK number ones with 'Everything I Own'?

3. Of whom did Fanny Brice say: 'Wet she's a star. Dry, she ain't'?

4. Which American singer was once ranked joint 85th in the world for the high jump?

5. What was the name of golfer Peter Alliss's father who played in three Ryder Cups for Britain?

6. Ponce is an industrial port in which country?

7. Peace, Just Joey and Whisky Mac are all varieties of what?

8. Michael Savage was Prime Minister of which country from 1935 to 1940?

9. Which BBC newsreader sat on a protesting lesbian during a 1988 invasion of the *Six O'Clock News* studio?

10. What was the name of the mistress who caused Cecil Parkinson's downfall?

11. In which decade was the first series of *The House of Eliot* set?

12. Which channel separates Sicily from Italy?

13. Which actress spent a month in a Rome prison in 1982 over income tax irregularities?

14. Which is the only bird with nostrils at the tip of its beak?

15. Which poet wrote *The Song of Hiawatha*?

16. Which phrase means 'it does not follow' in Latin?

Answers to page 105
QUIZ 104: **1.** *It'll Be Alright on the Night* **2.** 1920s **3.** Egypt **4.** A freshwater fish **5.** Sir Alec Douglas-Home **6.** Cheshire **7.** Green **8.** Worcestershire **9.** Huron **10.** Charles Darwin **11.** 18th **12.** Barry **13.** Norway **14.** Colin Blunstone **15.** Francis Ford Coppola **16.** Germany

Quiz 103

Answers on page 102

1. Which former child star was working as a painter and decorator ten years after being nominated for an Oscar for his role in *Kramer vs Kramer*?

2. What nationality was Laszlo Biro, inventor of the ball-point pen?

3. Which German driver raced for Sauber in the 2001 Formula One World Championship?

4. On which lake was Donald Campbell killed in *Bluebird* while attempting to break the World Water Speed Record?

5. Who played Rowdy Yates in the TV Western *Rawhide* before moving on to Hollywood stardom?

6. Who was President of the Soviet Union from 1977 to 1982?

7. Who was the second person to set foot on the Moon?

8. What Duke was James I's favourite, George Villiers?

9. Which poet wrote *Kubla Khan* and *The Ancient Mariner*?

10. Which sixties band used to be called Dean Ford and the Gaylords?

11. For which country's football team did a son replace his father during a 1996 international?

12. What was Bonnie Prince Charlie's full name?

13. What is the largest wild mammal native to Britain?

14. In which hemisphere is the Tropic of Capricorn?

15. Which trade name is derived from the Latin 'hominis vis', meaning 'strength of man'?

16. In which English county is Sir Thomas Tresham's Triangular Lodge?

Answers to page 102
QUIZ 101: **1.** Sky blue and white **2.** Decimalisation **3.** Paper clip **4.** 1981 **5.** Woodwind **6.** Judge Jeffreys **7.** Sweet **8.** Yellow **9.** Crimean War **10.** Glenda Jackson **11.** Portuguese **12.** Terry Hall **13.** Seahorse **14.** Cat **15.** Charles Bronson **16.** Marvin Rainwater

Quiz 104

Answers on page 103

1. Which TV programme celebrated only its 13th edition in 2001 even though it began in 1977?

2. In which decade did the Charleston become a popular dance?

3. Fuad I became king of which country from 1922?

4. What is a grayling?

5. Which former British Prime Minister once played first-class cricket for Middlesex?

6. In which English county is Jodrell Bank?

7. What colour was Roobarb the dog in *Roobarb and Custard*?

8. Which county cricket club have their headquarters at New Road?

9. Which is the second largest of the Great Lakes of North America?

10. Who published *On the Origin of Species* in 1859?

11. In which century did Samuel Pepys die?

12. Which boy's name means 'javelin'?

13. Which country stages an annual Grandmothers' Festival at Bodo in July?

14. Which singer didn't believe in miracles in 1972?

15. Who directed *The Godfather*?

16. Which country's football teams play in the Bundesliga?

Answers to page 103
QUIZ 102: **1.** Georges Pompidou **2.** Ken Boothe and Boy George **3.** Esther Williams **4.** Johnny Mathis **5.** Percy Alliss **6.** Puerto Rico **7.** Rose **8.** New Zealand **9.** Nicholas Witchell **10.** Sarah Keays **11.** 1920s **12.** Strait of Messina **13.** Sophia Loren **14.** Kiwi **15.** Henry Wadsworth Longfellow **16.** Non sequitur

Quiz 105

Answers on page 108

1. What happened in 1971 while Calgary's KFSM radio station was playing Carole King's 'I Feel the Earth Move'?

2. In which English county is the Isle of Purbeck?

3. Who wrote the children's story *The Old Man of Lochnagar*?

4. In which year did Cliff Richard reach number one in the UK with 'We Don't Talk Anymore'?

5. Who was joint manager of Charlton Athletic with Alan Curbishley?

6. Which is the most easterly of the Balearic Islands?

7. Which river links St Etienne and Nantes?

8. Charity Dingle is a character in which soap?

9. Fort Worth is a region of which American city?

10. According to legend, who saw above his head a sword suspended by a single hair?

11. What nationality was distance runner Emil Zátopek?

12. What is the term for the season when male deer become sexually aroused?

13. Who presents *Streetmate*?

14. Who is the builder on *Ground Force*?

15. Which is further north – Madrid, Valencia or Barcelona?

16. Who went solo after appearing in *The Partridge Family*?

Answers to page 108
QUIZ 107: **1.** Greg Rusedski **2.** Rome **3.** George Sand **4.** San Marino **5.** Ballet **6.** Spain **7.** The Boo Radleys **8.** 1996 **9.** Birmingham **10.** The jawbone **11.** Lebanon **12.** A jiffy **13.** A parrot-like bird **14.** Bears **15.** Romania **16.** Berkshire

Quiz 106

Answers on page 109

1. Which awards were made of wood to conserve metal during the Second World War?

2. William Peter Blatty wrote which supernatural novel that became a 1973 box-office smash in the cinema?

3. In which year did Charles I become King of England?

4. Which new town in Buckinghamshire was created in 1967?

5. What were Bingo, Crossbow and Horlicks?

6. Which London racecourse closed in 1979?

7. What part of the body does a genuphobic fear?

8. How many hours are China ahead of the UK?

9. Which country was ruled by the House of Vasa from 1523 to 1654?

10. Who was Jimmy Carter's Vice-President?

11. What is the chemical symbol for aluminium?

12. What Latin phrase means 'time flies'?

13. What was Maigret's Christian name?

14. Who wrote *Volpone* and *The Alchemist*?

15. What country has the international vehicle index ROU?

16. What did Casey Jones drive?

Answers to page 109
QUIZ 108: **1.** Hell's Angels **2.** *Emmerdale* **3.** St Christopher **4.** Richmond **5.** Harry Chapin **6.** Derby County **7.** Headingley **8.** Australia **9.** They are the longest words that can be typed with only the left hand **10.** None **11.** Miss Piggy **12.** Po **13.** Tribbiani **14.** Mike Gatting **15.** Champion **16.** Michael Foot

Quiz 107

Answers on page 106

1. In 1997, who became the first British man to reach the world's top ten tennis rankings?

2. In which city is the Trevi fountain?

3. What was the pen name of Amandine Aurore Lucie Dupin?

4. Which tiny European country is divided up into nine castles?

5. What type of dancer is Lynn Seymour?

6. In which country is Santander?

7. Which indie band took their name from a character in the novel *To Kill a Mockingbird*?

8. In which year was football 'coming home' to England?

9. In which city is the Bull Ring Shopping Centre?

10. What is the hardest bone in the human body?

11. In which country was Keanu Reeves born?

12. What name is given to one-hundredth of a second?

13. What is a lory?

14. What can be spectacled, sun or black?

15. Carol I became the first king of which country in 1881?

16. Eton College is in which county?

Answers to page 106
QUIZ 105: **1.** The studio collapsed **2.** Dorset **3.** Prince Charles **4.** 1979 **5.** Steve Gritt **6.** Minorca **7.** Loire **8.** *Emmerdale* **9.** Dallas **10.** Damocles **11.** Czech **12.** Rutting **13.** Davina McCall **14.** Tommy Walsh **15.** Barcelona **16.** David Cassidy

Quiz 108

Answers on page 107

1. Which motor-cycle gangs divide themselves into chapters?

2. In which soap did the pub owner marry the vicar in 2001?

3. Who is the patron saint of travellers?

4. What town name has a castle in North Yorkshire and a park near London?

5. Who sang about the morning DJ from 'W-O-L-D'?

6. Which Midlands football club are nicknamed the 'Rams'?

7. Which English cricket ground has the Kirkstall Lane end?

8. In which country is the Nullarbor Plain?

9. What is significant about the words 'stewardesses' and 'reverberated'?

10. How many living descendants does Shakespeare have?

11. Which Muppet was banned from Turkish TV during religious festivals so that viewers wouldn't be offended by the sight of an 'unclean' animal?

12. On which river does Turin stand?

13. What is Joey's surname in *Friends*?

14. Which England cricket captain was forced to apologise to umpire Shakoor Rana after a row that halted play for a day in Pakistan?

15. Which 'Wonder Horse' had his own TV series?

16. Who did Chris Patten call 'a kind of walking obituary for the Labour Party'?

Answers to page 107
QUIZ 106: **1.** The Oscars **2.** *The Exorcist* **3.** 1625 **4.** Milton Keynes **5.** Operation code names from the Second World War **6.** Alexandra Park **7.** Knees **8.** Eight **9.** Sweden **10.** Walter Mondale **11.** Al **12.** Tempus fugit **13.** Jules **14.** Ben Jonson **15.** Uruguay **16.** A railroad locomotive

Quiz 109

Answers on page 112

1. Which Alastair is a member of the Channel 4 horse racing team?

2. The larva of which insect is known as a leatherjacket?

3. Tyre is a port in which country?

4. Who directed the 1978 film *Invasion of the Body Snatchers*?

5. In which month of the year does the Le Mans 24-Hour Race traditionally take place?

6. Which nation has Dzongkha as its official language?

7. Who was the Roman god of war?

8. Which football club used to be called Thames Ironworks?

9. In which country is Cluedo's Colonel Mustard known as Madame Curry?

10. The first sets of dentures were used in which century?

11. Which is the second-longest river in the world?

12. Who turned down the Oliver Reed role in the 1969 film *Women in Love* because of the nude wrestling scene with Alan Bates?

13. What species of animal is a vicuna?

14. Who became US President in 1928?

15. *Allium cepa* is the Latin name for which vegetable?

16. Who had sixties hits with 'Zabadak' and 'The Legend of Xanadu'?

Answers to page 112

QUIZ 111: **1.** *Carry On Cowboy* **2.** Conway Twitty **3.** John Constable **4.** Corrugated iron **5.** 1961 **6.** Heard Island **7.** Melbourne **8.** 13th **9.** Pollux **10.** Idris the dragon **11.** Jonathan Aitken **12.** Gatwick **13.** Holby **14.** Spencer Tracy **15.** Astronomer Royal **16.** Thomas

Quiz 110

Answers on page 113

1. What bird is also known as the 'butcher-bird'?

2. Which town is the administrative headquarters of Shropshire?

3. At which battle was James, Duke of Monmouth, defeated in 1685 as he tried to seize the English throne?

4. What was the Christian name of the newspaper cartoonist Lancaster?

5. Which Hollywood actor was born Roy Scherer Jnr?

6. What did Alfred Cruickshank claim to have seen in 1923?

7. What do Jim Bowen and Franz Schubert have in common?

8. Who became Chancellor of the Exchequer in 1990?

9. What nationality was naturalist Carolus Linnaeus?

10. HKJ is the international index mark for vehicles in which country?

11. Which girl's name means 'serpent'?

12. Who was President of France from 1981 to 1995?

13. Which sixties pop star played Len Fairclough's son Stanley in *Coronation Street*?

14. In Argentine currency, how many australes are there in a peso?

15. Which country's national anthem is 'Inno di Mameli'?

16. What was 19 October 1987 otherwise known as in financial circles?

Answers to page 113
QUIZ 112: **1.** Elton John **2.** West Bromwich Albion **3.** The Flagellants **4.** One-sixteenth **5.** Michael Miles **6.** Johnny Rotten **7.** Burt Lancaster **8.** Dublin **9.** Flodden **10.** Two shillings **11.** 1947 **12.** Medea **13.** Norfolk **14.** Barbie **15.** Anne of Cleves **16.** Arnold Schönberg

Quiz 111

Answers on page 110

1. In which *Carry On* film did Richard O'Brien (of *Rocky Horror Show* fame) appear as an extra?

2. Which fifties singer changed his name from Harold Jenkins?

3. Who painted *The Hay Wain*?

4. What material did Frenchman Pierre Carpentier invent in 1853?

5. In which year did Yuri Gagarin become the first man in space?

6. On which island is the volcanic mountain Big Ben?

7. In which city were the 1956 Olympic Games staged?

8. In which century did Marco Polo first travel to China?

9. In Greek mythology, who was the twin brother of Castor?

10. Who lived in Ivor the Engine's boiler?

11. Who said of Margaret Thatcher: 'I wouldn't say she is open-minded on the Middle East, so much as empty-headed. She probably thinks Sinai is the plural of sinus'?

12. Where was the Grand National run between 1916 and 1918?

13. In which fictional town is *Casualty* set?

14. Who starred in *Bad Day at Black Rock* and *Guess Who's Coming to Dinner*?

15. Which title was John Flamsteed the first to hold, in 1675?

16. What was the Christian name of the furniture designer Chippendale?

Answers to page 110
QUIZ 109: **1.** Alastair Down **2.** Crane-fly **3.** Lebanon **4.** Philip Kaufman **5.** June **6.** Bhutan **7.** Mars **8.** West Ham United **9.** Switzerland **10.** 16th **11.** Amazon **12.** Michael Caine **13.** Llama **14.** Herbert Hoover **15.** Onion **16.** Dave Dee, Dozy, Beaky, Mick and Tich

Quiz 112

Answers on page 111

1. Which singer released a 1974 album titled *Caribou*?

2. Who won the 1968 FA Cup Final?

3. Which religious group whipped themselves into a frenzy in the Middle Ages?

4. What fraction of an ounce is equal to a dram?

5. Who originally presented the TV quiz *Take Your Pick*?

6. Who called Billy Idol 'the Perry Como of punk'?

7. Which Hollywood actor was born Stephen Burton?

8. Which capital city means 'black pool'?

9. At which battle of 1513 was King James IV of Scotland killed?

10. In pre-decimalisation currency, how much was a florin worth?

11. In which year did India achieve independence from Britain?

12. In Greek mythology, who was the sorceress daughter of the King of Colchis?

13. In which English county is Thetford?

14. Which female icon was created by Ruth Handler in 1959?

15. Who was known as 'The Flanders Mare'?

16. Which Austrian-born composer, who was superstitious about the number 13, died on Friday the 13th at 13 minutes to midnight?

Answers to page 111
QUIZ 110: **1.** Shrike **2.** Shrewsbury **3.** Sedgemoor **4.** Osbert **5.** Rock Hudson **6.** Loch Ness Monster **7.** They were both schoolteachers **8.** Norman Lamont **9.** Swedish **10.** Jordan **11.** Linda **12.** François Mitterrand **13.** Peter Noone (Herman's Hermits) **14.** 10,000 **15.** Italy **16.** Black Monday

Quiz 113

Answers on page 116

1. What was the stage name of singer Asa Yoelson?

2. What did women in America start burning in 1970?

3. In which city is the Bosporus suspension bridge?

4. What nationality was skier Alberto Tomba?

5. Cathy McGowan made her name on which TV show?

6. What residents of Trafalgar Square were created by Edwin Landseer?

7. Who directed the 1999 movie *Eyes Wide Shut*?

8. Which food is traditionally used to ward off vampires?

9. Which former *Big Breakfast* presenter is the daughter of a comedian?

10. With which country is the fondue most associated?

11. What is the capital of Croatia?

12. Who directed the 1993 film *A Bronx Tale*?

13. What does a postilion ride?

14. Which European landmark has 1,792 steps?

15. Which band urged you to 'Sit Down'?

16. The Kattegat lies to the east of which country?

Answers to page 116
QUIZ 115: **1.** Lord Snowdon **2.** Hectometres **3.** Frank Marker **4.** Purple **5.** Northern Line
6. Nottingham **7.** London **8.** Hanging **9.** Brian de Palma **10.** 16th **11.** *M*A*S*H* **12.** Fly-half
13. Flea **14.** Anemone **15.** Hans Christian Andersen **16.** Wild sheep

Quiz 114

Answers on page 117

1. What is dulse?

2. Which breed of dog shares its name with a coastal region of Canada?

3. Which bear celebrated his 70th birthday in 1996?

4. Which country's currency is the real?

5. On which island is the Mauna Loa volcano?

6. In Chinese theory, what is the opposite of yin?

7. How many questions must be answered correctly to win the jackpot on *Who Wants To Be a Millionaire*?

8. Who composed the *Fingal's Cave* overture?

9. Which American driver won the Formula One World Championship in 1978?

10. Which animal strolled down the street at the start of each episode of *Northern Exposure*?

11. In what field of photography did Eric Hosking specialise?

12. What figure is Cerne Abbas famous for?

13. Which university crew has clocked up the most wins in the Boat Race?

14. Which footballing nation won the 1976 European Championship?

15. In which book does *The Wife of Bath's Tale* appear?

16. What are dolly, dimmer and rocker?

Answers to page 117
QUIZ 116: **1.** Busby Berkeley **2.** *Play Your Cards Right* **3.** Pacific **4.** A large grouse **5.** West Midlands **6.** Canon **7.** 11th **8.** Common Agricultural Policy **9.** 'Downtown Train' **10.** Golf **11.** Argentina **12.** Skin disorders **13.** Una Stubbs and Lionel Blair **14.** Rod Steiger **15.** Israel **16.** 13

Quiz 115

Answers on page 114

1. Which former member of the royal family designed an aviary at London Zoo?

2. What are there ten of in a kilometre?

3. Who was the shabby private detective hero in the TV series *Public Eye*?

4. What colour was Sheb Wooley's Flying People Eater?

5. Morden is at the southern end of which London Underground line?

6. In which city was the royal standard raised at the start of the English Civil War?

7. Which city had the world's largest population in 1900?

8. What was abolished in Britain in December 1969?

9. Who directed *Carrie* and *The Untouchables*?

10. In which century was curling first played?

11. 'Suicide Is Painless' was the theme song to which TV series?

12. In what position did Rob Andrew play rugby for England?

13. Which insect can jump 200 times its own height?

14. What is another name for the windflower?

15. Who wrote *The Ugly Duckling* and *The Little Mermaid*?

16. What is an argali?

Answers to page 114
QUIZ 113: **1.** Al Jolson **2.** Their bras **3.** Istanbul **4.** Italian **5.** *Ready, Steady, Go!* **6.** The lions at the foot of Nelson's Column **7.** Stanley Kubrick **8.** Garlic **9.** Liza Tarbuck (daughter of Jimmy) **10.** Switzerland **11.** Zagreb **12.** Robert De Niro **13.** A horse **14.** Eiffel Tower **15.** James **16.** Denmark

Quiz 116

Answers on page 115

1. What stage name was used by choreographer William Berkeley Enos?

2. What was the American TV game show *Card Sharks* called when it moved to the UK?

3. In which ocean is the Bismarck Archipelago?

4. What is a blackcock?

5. The Black Country is in which area of England?

6. What can be an echo form in music or a type of priest?

7. In which century was Canterbury Cathedral begun?

8. In the European Union, what does CAP stand for?

9. Which Tom Waits song was a hit for Rod Stewart?

10. At what sport was Peter Oosterhuis a professional?

11. What country boasts the highest and lowest spots in South America?

12. What is dermatology the treatment of?

13. Who were the original team captains on *Give Us a Clue*?

14. Which actor's films included *On the Waterfront* and *The Pawnbroker*?

15. Where is the plain of Sharon?

16. How many popes have been Innocent?

Answers to page 115
QUIZ 114: **1.** An edible seaweed **2.** Labrador **3.** Winnie the Pooh **4.** Brazil **5.** Hawaii **6.** Yang **7.** 15 **8.** Mendelssohn **9.** Mario Andretti **10.** Moose **11.** Wildlife **12.** Giant **13.** Cambridge **14.** Czechoslovakia **15.** *Canterbury Tales* **16.** Types of light switches

Quiz 117

Answers on page 120

1. What is the state capital of Delaware?

2. What bird is the symbol of the United States?

3. Which sitcom starred Richard Beckinsale and Paula Wilcox as Geoffrey and Beryl?

4. What is an animal without a backbone called?

5. Which explorer has the middle name Twistleton-Wykeham?

6. Which style of architecture is distinguished by vertical lines of tall pillars, and by pointed arches?

7. How many gold medals did swimmer Mark Spitz win at the 1972 Olympics?

8. In which year did Sir Winston Churchill die?

9. Who was Poet Laureate from 1930 to 1968?

10. Who was the last King of Austria?

11. Which children's TV presenter released records as Bombalurina?

12. In which country does the Henley-on-Todd Regatta take place?

13. With which football team did Angus Deayton have trials?

14. What is rolled down Cooper's Hill in Gloucestershire?

15. Where are your metatarsals?

16. In which play did Mrs Malaprop first appear?

Answers to page 120
QUIZ 119: **1.** Bruce Lee **2.** Sedgefield **3.** Black, red and gold **4.** Balaclava **5.** Claude **6.** Great Wall of China **7.** Gabon **8.** Vancouver **9.** Shoulder Pork and hAM **10.** Henry Cooper **11.** Passenger pigeon **12.** Buckeye State **13.** Antarctica **14.** Cassandra **15.** Harold Macmillan **16.** Stravinsky

Quiz 118

Answers on page 121

1. What nationality is the film director Milos Forman?

2. In which county did the north-bound M1 end when it opened in 1959?

3. Which former member of The Shadows was electrocuted by his guitar?

4. Which country are the reigning Olympic rugby union champions?

5. Roughly how many islands make up the Hebrides – 100, 300, 500?

6. Which three countries make up Benelux?

7. Who did Jimmy Carter defeat in the 1976 US Presidential election?

8. What is the Chilean pine tree commonly known as?

9. What was the name of the British policewoman killed in the 1984 Libyan embassy protest?

10. Which TV sitcom originated from a stage play called *The Banana Box*?

11. Which poet and garden designer was married to Harold Nicolson?

12. In which year was the General Strike?

13. What is the world's oldest classic horse race?

14. What links Cliff Richard and Vivien Leigh?

15. What is a common spadefoot?

16. Which Irish novelist won the 1993 Booker Prize?

Answers to page 121
QUIZ 120: **1.** Radio Caroline **2.** Michael Fagan **3.** Eucalyptus shoots **4.** Magna Carta **5.** Colonel Blood **6.** Minehead **7.** Spencer Davis Group **8.** Garrincha **9.** Cornflower **10.** Fauvism **11.** 1973 **12.** Anzac Day **13.** Jarvis Cocker **14.** Mr Motivator **15.** Rochdale **16.** Alistair MacLean

Quiz 119

Answers on page 118

1. Which star died during filming of his movie, *Game of Death,* in 1973?

2. For which constituency is Tony Blair the MP?

3. Which three colours are in Germany's national flag?

4. During which battle did the ill-fated Charge of the Light Brigade take place?

5. What was Debussy's Christian name?

6. Which edifice was built on the orders of Shih Huang Ti?

7. Libreville is the capital of which African country?

8. In which city is the Lion's Gate Bridge?

9. What does Spam stand for?

10. Which boxer starred as prizefighter John Gully in the 1975 film *Royal Flash*?

11. Which bird, one of the commonest in the world in 1814, became extinct a century later?

12. What is the nickname of the American state of Ohio?

13. In which continent is Mount Erebus?

14. Which yuppie banker did Rodney marry in *Only Fools and Horses*?

15. Who told electors in 1959: 'You've never had it so good'?

16. Who composed 'The Firebird'?

Answers to page 118
QUIZ 117: **1.** Dover **2.** Eagle **3.** *The Lovers* **4.** An invertebrate **5.** Sir Ranulph Fiennes **6.** Gothic
7. Seven **8.** 1965 **9.** John Masefield **10.** Karl I **11.** Timmy Mallett **12.** Australia **13.** Crystal Palace
14. Cheese **15.** In your feet **16.** *The Rivals*

Quiz 120

Answers on page 119

1. Which was Britain's first pirate radio station?

2. Who broke into the Queen's bedroom in 1982?

3. What is the staple diet of the koala bear?

4. What was signed on 15 June 1215?

5. Which Irish adventurer attempted to steal the Crown Jewels from the Tower of London in 1671?

6. Which resort is located at the north-eastern edge of Exmoor?

7. Which group had a number one hit in 1966 with 'Keep On Running'?

8. Which Brazilian footballer was nicknamed 'Little Bird'?

9. Which plant has the Latin name *Centaurea cyanus*?

10. Which art movement originated in Paris in 1905 with the founding of the Salon d'Automne?

11. In which year did the UK join the European Union?

12. 25 April is which national holiday in Australia and New Zealand?

13. Who once interrupted Michael Jackson's stage performance at the Brit Awards?

14. As whom was TV fitness expert Derrick Evans better known?

15. Which football club plays at Spotland?

16. Which novelist wrote *The Guns of Navarone*, *Ice Station Zebra* and *Where Eagles Dare*?

Answers to page 119
QUIZ 118: **1.** Czech **2.** Northamptonshire **3.** John Rostill **4.** USA (they took gold in 1924 when rugby union was last an Olympic sport) **5.** 500 **6.** Belgium, the Netherlands and Luxembourg **7.** Gerald Ford **8.** Monkey puzzle **9.** Yvonne Fletcher **10.** *Rising Damp* **11.** Vita Sackville-West **12.** 1926 **13.** St Leger **14.** Both were born in India **15.** A European toad **16.** Roddy Doyle

Quiz 121

Answers on page 124

1. On which island is Ronaldsway Airport?

2. Who was Gerald Ford's Vice-President?

3. At what age does a filly become a mare?

4. From which country are the band Midnight Oil?

5. What is the US equivalent of a post code?

6. Who directed *Lock, Stock and Two Smoking Barrels*?

7. In the NATO phonetic alphabet, which word represents the letter 'G'?

8. In *A Tale of Two Cities*, who was Sidney Carton's doppelganger?

9. Which bird was on the reverse side of the last farthing?

10. Who wrote *Brighton Rock* and *Monsignor Quixote*?

11. Who played Cruella de Vil in *101 Dalmatians*?

12. Who captained the British Lions rugby team on their triumphant tour to South Africa in 1974?

13. Which early film comedian was noted for his trademark horn-rimmed glasses and straw hat?

14. Llandrindod Wells is the administrative headquarters of which county?

15. In which ocean is the Sargasso Sea?

16. What name is given to the widow of a king?

Answers to page 124
QUIZ 123: **1.** Eight **2.** Fish **3.** A bird **4.** Agent Cooper in *Twin Peaks* **5.** One Thousand Guineas
6. 'Nasty Nigel' **7.** Edinburgh **8.** Jeroboam **9.** Special Air Service **10.** Elgin City and Peterhead
11. Jaw **12.** Ruff **13.** Paris **14.** Giant panda **15.** Alan Jones **16.** Rubber plant

Quiz 122

Answers on page 125

1. What is the equivalent of the Red Cross in Muslim countries?

2. In which country is Linate Airport?

3. Mrs Danvers is the sinister housekeeper in which novel?

4. What did Trevor Chappell do in 1980 to prevent New Zealand winning a Test match against Australia?

5. Which zoo is situated north-east of Tamworth?

6. What was the name of Prince Edward's TV production company?

7. Hamlet was the prince of which country?

8. Who played Queen Elizabeth I in *Blackadder II*?

9. The Heartbreakers backed which American singer?

10. Which Nightingale reads the ITV news?

11. St Peter Port is the capital of which of the Channel Islands?

12. Which British national newspaper folded in 1971?

13. Which minister earned the nickname 'Milk Snatcher' after abolishing free milk for schoolchildren?

14. Which African country's national coach was banned from football for life by the king after the team were eliminated from the 1998 World Cup qualifiers by Kenya?

15. What is the capital of Belarus?

16. Which movie directed by Robert Redford won the Oscar for Best Picture in 1980?

Answers to page 125
QUIZ 124: **1.** The Eagles **2.** *One Man and His Dog* **3.** Dickie Bird **4.** All three were Hollywood actors born in Vancouver, Canada **5.** Woody Allen **6.** Sigourney Weaver **7.** 'Relax' **8.** George I **9.** Kentucky **10.** Felix **11.** Leicester City **12.** Lee Kuan Yew **13.** Australia **14.** Ray Stubbs **15.** China, Laos and Cambodia **16.** Saigon

Quiz 123

Answers on page 122

1. How many legs do spiders have?

2. With which food is London's Billingsgate Market associated?

3. What is a spoonbill?

4. Which TV agent had a thing about cherry pie?

5. In horse racing, which of the Guineas is for fillies only?

6. What nickname did TV executive Nigel Lythgoe earn after his appearances as a judge on *Popstars*?

7. In which city is Murrayfield Stadium?

8. What name is given to a wine bottle four times the ordinary size?

9. In military parlance, what does SAS stand for?

10. Which two football clubs were elected to the Scottish League in 2000?

11. Whereabouts in the human body is the maxilla?

12. Which bird gets its name from the frill of feathers around the neck of the male?

13. Which European city is famous for its Latin quarter?

14. Which animal can eat almost 100lb of bamboo shoots in a single day?

15. Which Australian was Formula One World Champion in 1980?

16. Which house plant has the Latin name *Ficus elastica*?

Answers to page 122
QUIZ 121: **1.** Isle of Man **2.** Nelson Rockefeller **3.** Four **4.** Australia **5.** Zip code **6.** Guy Ritchie
7. Golf **8.** Charles Darnay **9.** Wren **10.** Graham Greene **11.** Glenn Close **12.** Willie John McBride
13. Harold Lloyd **14.** Powys **15.** Atlantic **16.** Dowager

Quiz 124

Answers on page 123

1. Don Henley is the drummer with which band?

2. Katy Cropper was the first woman to win which TV competition?

3. Which chirpy cricket umpire retired from the game in 1998?

4. What do Yvonne De Carlo, Michael J. Fox and Barbara Parkins have in common?

5. Who said of death: 'There is the fear that there is an afterlife but no one will know where it's being held'?

6. Which actress chose her first name from a character in the novel *The Great Gatsby*?

7. Which 1983 song shot to the top of the charts after Radio 1 DJ Mike Read announced that he was refusing to play it because of its sexual content?

8. Which English king was known as 'The Turnip-Hoer'?

9. In which American state is Fort Knox?

10. Which cartoon cat was created by Pat Sullivan in 1919?

11. Peter Taylor managed which Premiership football club at the start of the 2001–2 season?

12. Who was Prime Minister of Singapore from 1959 to 1990?

13. Wattle is the national flower of which country?

14. Which former Tranmere Rovers full-back is part of the BBC's soccer team?

15. Which three countries border Vietnam?

16. What was the former name of Ho Chi Minh City?

Answers to page 123

QUIZ 122: **1.** The Red Crescent **2.** Italy **3.** *Rebecca* **4.** He bowled underarm along the ground **5.** Twycross **6.** Ardent **7.** Denmark **8.** Miranda Richardson **9.** Tom Petty **10.** Mary Nightingale **11.** Guernsey **12.** *Daily Sketch* **13.** Margaret Thatcher **14.** Algeria **15.** Minsk **16.** *Ordinary People*

Quiz 125

Answers on page 128

1. Slide Mountain is the highest peak in which US mountain range?

2. Which river flows through Chester?

3. What did Charlie Chan call his eldest offspring, Barry?

4. In 1967, which golfer made the first televised hole-in-one?

5. Which is the smallest native British deer?

6. Which monster in Greek mythology had nine heads?

7. Jomo Kenyatta became the first President of which country in 1964?

8. What was Edwin Lutyens by profession?

9. Who released the 1997 album *OK Computer*?

10. What was significant about footballer Mo Johnston's transfer to Rangers in 1989?

11. Who directed *Women in Love* and *The Devils*?

12. Which Hollywood actress was born Caryn Johnson?

13. Who designed the Clifton Suspension Bridge?

14. What colour are the flowers of a celandine?

15. Who was the first English printer?

16. Who was the commander of *Stingray*?

Answers to page 128
QUIZ 127: **1.** David 'Kid' Jensen **2.** Thomas Hardy **3.** Mississippi **4.** Worzel Gummidge **5.** Ryder Cup **6.** Gary Hart **7.** In your ear **8.** Goldcrest **9.** Australia **10.** King Lear **11.** Liverpool **12.** Five **13.** Mickey Mouse ('Life is a Minestrone') **14.** Botticelli **15.** Tom Finney **16.** South Island

Quiz 126

Answers on page 129

1. From which country did the chow dog originate?

2. What is the name of the area of low atmospheric pressure along the equator where calm winds can suddenly produce storms?

3. What two colours make up the flag of Portugal?

4. What was the Christian name of the German car designer Porsche?

5. On which ground do the Scotland rugby union team play home matches?

6. As which sixties pop star did Reg Balls re-invent himself?

7. Muskie and Vince assisted which law enforcer?

8. Eboracum was the Roman name for which city?

9. What piece of furniture is a chesterfield?

10. Scottish blackface and cheviot are breeds of which animal?

11. Chesil Beach is in which English county?

12. Who went from playing a brickie to wearing 'Crocodile Shoes'?

13. Which south-coast resort is host to a pre-Wimbledon tennis tournament?

14. What was the middle name of the poet Percy Shelley?

15. Which Independent candidate fought unsuccessfully against Bill Clinton in the 1992 US Presidential campaign?

16. Who is Wayne Slob's wife?

Answers to page 129
QUIZ 128: **1.** Italian **2.** Albania **3.** A hairy-leaved plant **4.** Sandown Park **5.** Duran Duran **6.** Michael Caine (*The Caine Mutiny*) **7.** Philip II **8.** Sykes **9.** Jordan **10.** Screaming Lord Sutch **11.** Australasia **12.** Tom Wolfe **13.** Calista Flockhart **14.** Harry Vardon **15.** Elizabeth I **16.** Coldplay

Quiz 127

Answers on page 126

1. Which former Radio 1 disc jockey is a descendant of Robert Louis Stevenson?

2. Who wrote *Far from the Madding Crowd*?

3. Which US state is known as the 'Magnolia State'?

4. Who lived in Ten Acre Field at Scatterbrook Farm?

5. In 1985, what did Europe regain for the first time in 28 years?

6. Who withdrew from the 1988 US Presidential race following newspaper revelations about his relationship with model Donna Rice?

7. Where would you find your hammer, anvil and stirrup?

8. What is the smallest British bird?

9. In which country is the Gibson Desert?

10. Whose daughters were Goneril and Regan?

11. Which English football team achieved a European and domestic treble in 2001?

12. How many lines are there in a limerick?

13. According to 10cc, who gets more fan mail than the Pope?

14. Which 15th-century Italian artist's name means 'little barrel'?

15. Which former England international footballer was known as the 'Preston plumber'?

16. On which island of New Zealand is the city of Christchurch?

Answers to page 126
QUIZ 125: **1.** The Catskills **2.** Dee **3.** 'Number One Son' **4.** Tony Jacklin **5.** Roe deer **6.** Hydra **7.** Kenya **8.** Architect **9.** Radiohead **10.** He was Rangers' first Catholic signing **11.** Ken Russell **12.** Whoopi Goldberg **13.** Isambard Kingdom Brunel **14.** Yellow **15.** William Caxton **16.** Troy Tempest

Quiz 128

Answers on page 127

1. What nationality was Christopher Columbus?

2. In the currency of which country do 100 qindarka make a lek?

3. What is comfrey?

4. On which racecourse is the Whitbread Gold Cup run?

5. Which band took their name from the villain in the film *Barbarella*?

6. Which actor took his stage name from a Humphrey Bogart movie?

7. Which Spanish king despatched the Armada?

8. Who lived at 24 Sebastopol Terrace, Acton?

9. Which Formula One team sacked driver Heinz-Harald Frentzen halfway through the 2001 season?

10. Who formed the National Teenage Party in 1963?

11. In which continent does the wombat live?

12. Who wrote the novel *The Bonfire of the Vanities?*

13. Who plays Ally McBeal?

14. Who was the first British golfer to win the US Open?

15. Who was the last Tudor monarch?

16. Which band had hits with 'Yellow' and 'Trouble'?

Answers to page 127
QUIZ 126: **1.** China **2.** Doldrums **3.** Green and red **4.** Ferdinand **5.** Murrayfield **6.** Reg Presley **7.** Deputy Dawg **8.** York **9.** Sofa **10.** Sheep **11.** Dorset **12.** Jimmy Nail **13.** Eastbourne **14.** Bysshe **15.** Ross Perot **16.** Waynetta

Quiz 129

Answers on page 132

1. Which distance runner was known as the Flying Finn?

2. Whose 2001 album was titled *Songs From the West Coast*?

3. Which rival TV cook labelled Jamie Oliver's shows 'tacky and gimmicky'?

4. What is the nickname of Northampton rugby club?

5. Who played Virginia Woolf in the 2003 movie *The Hours*?

6. In which ocean is the Gulf of Ob?

7. Who starred as Lawrence of Arabia in the 1962 film of that title?

8. Who got in a basket with Teddy and Andy Pandy?

9. In which town is the ground of Grimsby Town Football Club?

10. In which city did the Peterloo massacre take place?

11. The ringgit is the currency of which country?

12. What number American President is George W. Bush?

13. Who played the devil in the remake of the film *Bedazzled*?

14. In 1996, who became the first British tennis player for 23 years to reach the quarter-finals of the men's singles at Wimbledon?

15. On which river does the Yorkshire town of Halifax stand?

16. Which Hollywood beauty made her film debut in *The Mask*?

Answers to page 132
QUIZ 131: **1.** Terrier **2.** Tina Turner **3.** Southern lights **4.** Coventry City **5.** Scarborough **6.** The Proms **7.** Bowls **8.** Donna **9.** Robbie Williams **10.** George Patton **11.** Pay-As-You-Earn **12.** Eddie Murphy **13.** Morrissey **14.** Buckingham Palace **15.** The Moby **16.** Maastricht Treaty

Quiz 130

Answers on page 133

1. Which singer married choreographer Cris Judd in 2001?

2. Which country borders Kenya to the south?

3. In 1994, who was sworn in as the first black President of South Africa?

4. Which Lancashire cricketer was appointed England captain in 1993?

5. Who did Boy George become on *Stars in Their Eyes*?

6. Which race traditionally ends at Mortlake?

7. Who created the Secret Seven?

8. Which actor wrote *A Short Walk From Harrods* in 1993?

9. Pablo Casals became famous for playing which musical instrument?

10. Who was 'Livin' La Vida Loca'?

11. In which country did the Boxer Rebellion take place?

12. What did Dick Whittington achieve that Jeffrey Archer didn't?

13. Which flower became a craze in 17th-century Holland?

14. Which town provides the Scottish mainland terminus for the steamer service to the Orkneys?

15. Which river forms a long stretch of the border between Devon and Cornwall?

16. The Gulf of San Matias is off the coast of which country?

Answers to page 133
QUIZ 132: **1.** Cheshire **2.** Flashing directional indicator lights **3.** Denmark **4.** Four **5.** Maria Callas **6.** Charles Dance **7.** Boccaccio **8.** Leonardo DiCaprio **9.** Baha Men **10.** Dry ice **11.** Kew **12.** Nigel Kennedy **13.** Puck **14.** Sarajevo **15.** Swedish **16.** Larry Grayson

Quiz 131

Answers on page 130

1. Sealyham is a breed of which type of dog?

2. Which singer was born Annie Mae Bullock?

3. What is the common name for Aurora australis?

4. Which Football League club plays at Highfield Road?

5. What is the home town of playwright Alan Ayckbourn?

6. Which series of concerts was founded by Henry Wood?

7. What game was Sir Francis Drake playing as the Spanish Armada approached?

8. What was the name of Dave Tucker's feisty wife in *Soldier, Soldier*?

9. 'Rock DJ' was a huge hit for which singer?

10. Which US general was known as 'Old Blood and Guts'?

11. What does PAYE stand for?

12. Who starred in *Vampire in Brooklyn* and *The Nutty Professor*?

13. Whose solo albums have included *Viva Hate* and *Your Arsenal*?

14. Marble Arch was constructed originally as a ceremonial entrance to which building?

15. What was the name of Ron Dixon's mobile shop in *Brookside*?

16. Which treaty was drawn up by European Community heads in 1991?

Answers to page 130
QUIZ 129: **1.** Paavo Nurmi **2.** Elton John **3.** Antonio Carluccio **4.** 'The Saints' **5.** Nicole Kidman **6.** Arctic Ocean **7.** Peter O'Toole **8.** Looby Loo **9.** Cleethorpes **10.** Manchester **11.** Malaysia **12.** 43rd **13.** Liz Hurley **14.** Tim Henman **15.** Calder **16.** Cameron Diaz

Quiz 132

Answers on page 131

1. In which county are Warrington and Widnes?

2. What were made compulsory on cars in Britain in 1954?

3. Which was the first country to introduce VAT?

4. How many Epsom Derby winners did Willie Carson ride?

5. Which singer was born Maria Kalogeropoulos?

6. Who played Guy Perron in *The Jewel in the Crown*?

7. Who wrote *The Decameron*?

8. Which actor made his movie debut as Tobias Wolff in *This Boy's Life*?

9. 'Who Let the Dogs Out' in 2000?

10. What is another name for solid carbon dioxide, often used in stage shows?

11. Where are London's Royal Botanic Gardens?

12. Whose 1986 recording of Vivaldi's 'Four Seasons' sold over a million copies?

13. What is used in place of a ball in ice hockey?

14. Where was Archduke Franz Ferdinand assassinated in 1914 – the event which sparked the First World War?

15. What nationality is tennis player Mats Wilander?

16. Who succeeded Bruce Forsyth in the seventies as host of *The Generation Game*?

Answers to page 131
QUIZ 130: **1.** Jennifer Lopez **2.** Tanzania **3.** Nelson Mandela **4.** Mike Atherton **5.** David Bowie's Ziggy Stardust **6.** The Boat Race **7.** Enid Blyton **8.** Dirk Bogarde **9.** Cello **10.** Ricky Martin **11.** China **12.** Lord Mayor of London **13.** Tulip **14.** Thurso **15.** Tamar **16.** Argentina

Quiz 133

Answers on page 136

1. Which is the only ten-letter word that can be spelt just using the top row of letters of a keyboard?

2. In which state is Detroit?

3. Who was the first English king from the House of Lancaster?

4. The okapi is a member of which animal family?

5. Which were the five original Cinque Ports?

6. In which country could you buy a chocolate bar called Plopp?

7. The Isis is the upper stretch of which English river?

8. Which Spanish rider won the Tour de France five years in a row from 1991 to 1995?

9. Which knight of the stage played his last-ever role, as a pub landlord in Paul McCartney's film *Give My Regards to Broad Street*?

10. As whom is Marvin Lee Aday better known?

11. Which football club held the FA Cup for eight years even though they won it only once?

12. What is a dugong?

13. Which Chinese dynasty began in AD 618 and ended in 907?

14. In which English county is Gotham?

15. How many points are scored by kicking the ball into the net in Gaelic football?

16. Who was the subject of the Neil Sedaka song 'Oh Carol'?

Answers to page 136
QUIZ 135: **1.** Chile **2.** Stamford Bridge **3.** Ben Turpin **4.** Oscar Wilde **5.** Madrid **6.** Alexander Fleming **7.** Holland **8.** Leila Williams **9.** 'Some Might Say' **10.** Crippen **11.** Ecuador **12.** A turnip **13.** Gloucestershire **14.** The Nobel Prize for Chemistry **15.** Norway **16.** 1982

Quiz 134

Answers on page 137

1. In which English county is Biggin Hill Airport?

2. What is the international vehicle index mark for Israel?

3. Who said: 'Hey, don't knock masturbation! It's sex with someone I love!'

4. Which law enforcers made their first appearance in London in 1960?

5. What was Bodie's first name in *The Professionals*?

6. Which letter do more capital cities start with than any other?

7. Approximately how many years ago did heated rollers first come into use for hair-styling?

8. Which Welsh town means 'Vale of the Crow'?

9. What colour are the flowers of the lily of the valley?

10. Of which political party was Benjamin Disraeli the leader?

11. What is 44 in Roman numerals?

12. What is the official language of Surinam?

13. Andy McCluskey and Paul Humphreys made up which eighties band?

14. Who created the priestly detective Father Brown?

15. Who was Henry VIII's fifth wife?

16. How did the Roman Emperor Claudius die?

Answers to page 137
QUIZ 136: **1.** Madonna **2.** Horse **3.** Western Australia **4.** An antelope **5.** Edgar Rice Burroughs
6. The FA Cup Final **7.** Nancy Spungen **8.** Clark Gable **9.** Flying mower **10.** Burglar alarm
11. Don Thompson (50km walk) **12.** *Amoco Cadiz* **13.** Dvořák **14.** Judy Garland **15.** Lithuania
16. Queen Victoria

Quiz 135

Answers on page 134

1. In which country is the Atacama Desert?

2. What name links a London football ground with an 11th-century battle on English soil?

3. Which silent movie star was insured for $100,000 against the possibility of his eyes ever becoming normal again?

4. Who wrote *Lady Windermere's Fan*?

5. *ABC* and *Ya* are national newspapers published in which European city?

6. Who discovered penicillin?

7. In which country was gin first produced?

8. Who was the first female presenter of *Blue Peter*?

9. What was the title of Oasis's first UK number one single?

10. Which notorious killer had the first names Hawley Harvey?

11. Which country owns the Galapagos Islands?

12. What did a Bolton Wanderers fan throw in front of Wolves manager Graham Taylor in 1995 to incur a £60 fine?

13. In which English county is the Forest of Dean?

14. What did Ahmed Zewail win in 1999?

15. Which Scandinavian country is not a member of the European Union?

16. In which year was the Falklands conflict?

Answers to page 134
QUIZ 133: **1.** Typewriter **2.** Michigan **3.** Henry IV **4.** Giraffe **5.** Sandwich, Dover, Hythe, Romney and Hastings **6.** Sweden **7.** Thames **8.** Miguel Indurain **9.** Sir Ralph Richardson **10.** Meat Loaf
11. Portsmouth (who won the Cup in 1939, the competition not resuming until after the war)
12. A marine mammal **13.** Tang **14.** Nottinghamshire **15.** Three **16.** Carole King

Quiz 136

Answers on page 135

1. Whose black bra fetched £4,600 at auction in 1997?

2. 2002 is the year of which animal in the Chinese calendar?

3. Which is the largest state in Australia?

4. What is a bushbuck?

5. Who wrote *Tarzan of the Apes*?

6. At which important event did Mr S.R. Bastard officiate in 1878?

7. What was the name of the girlfriend that The Sex Pistols' Sid Vicious was charged with murdering?

8. Which Hollywood star got his big break when, working as a telephone repair man, he went to mend the phone of drama coach Josephine Dillon who promptly took him under her wing?

9. What is 'Flymo' an abbreviation of?

10. Which safety device was invented by Edwin T. Holmes in 1858?

11. Who won Britain's only athletics gold medal at the 1960 Olympics?

12. Which tanker spilt over 200,000 tons of oil into the English Channel after drifting on to rocks off the coast of Brittany in 1978?

13. Who composed the 'New World Symphony'?

14. Which actress was born Frances Gumm?

15. Vilnius is the capital of which country?

16. Who was the last Hanoverian monarch to rule England?

Answers to page 135
QUIZ 134: **1.** Kent **2.** IL **3.** Woody Allen in *Annie Hall* **4.** Traffic wardens **5.** William **6.** B **7.** 4,000 (the ancient Egyptians used them) **8.** Cymbran **9.** White **10.** The Tories **11.** XLIV **12.** Dutch **13.** OMD **14.** G.K. Chesterton **15.** Catherine Howard **16.** He choked to death on a feather put down his throat by doctors to make him vomit

Quiz 137

Answers on page 140

1. Which fake was 'discovered' by Charles Dawson in East Sussex in 1913?

2. Which horror movie actor's real name was William Pratt?

3. The tiny rock hyrax – a rat-like creature from central Africa – is the closest living relative of which mammal?

4. Which nation's people eat more bread per person than anyone else in the world?

5. Which series was the successor to *That Was The Week That Was*?

6. Which New Zealand-born scientist was awarded the Nobel Prize for Chemistry in 1908?

7. About which cathedral did The New Vaudeville Band sing in 1966?

8. What was the name of the woodpecker in *Bagpuss*?

9. Which capital city means 'elephant's trunk'?

10. The Rye House Plot was a conspiracy against which English monarch?

11. Who led the Sioux onslaught against General Custer at the Battle of Little Big Horn?

12. What was U2's first UK number one single?

13. Which flowers have varieties called hybrid teas and floribundas?

14. What is the connection between dynamite and the Nobel Peace Prize?

15. What is the spiny anteater otherwise known as?

16. Which country owns Easter Island?

Answers to page 140
QUIZ 139: **1.** Vulture **2.** Timothy McVeigh **3.** Dover **4.** Melanie Chisholm **5.** Alexander Dubček
6. Australia **7.** Medway **8.** They've all had hip replacements **9.** Marlene Dietrich **10.** Belgium
11. Four **12.** Mrs Strickland **13.** Canadian **14.** Pacific **15.** Pandora **16.** An antelope-like mammal of the USA

Quiz 138

Answers on page 141

1. What was the name of Jed Clampett's daughter in *The Beverly Hillbillies*?

2. What wrecked the opening night of BBC2 in 1964?

3. In which year did Muhammad Ali first become World Heavyweight Boxing Champion?

4. Which novelist created detective Albert Campion?

5. The name of which sixties pop group means 'far from these things'?

6. What does the computer program language BASIC stand for?

7. Of which family of freshwater fish is the chub a member?

8. In soccer, which country staged the 1982 World Cup finals?

9. Which famous playboy was seen as a pipe-smoking ancient Roman in Mel Brooks' *History of the World – Part 1*?

10. Who invented the electric light bulb?

11. Who scored against his namesake in the 2001–2 Merseyside derby at Goodison Park?

12. Which American politician has a wife called Tipper?

13. Which spirit is the basic ingredient in the liqueur benedictine?

14. Which former TV weathergirl presented the game show *Dog Eat Dog*?

15. Which London building housed the Great Exhibition of 1851?

16. In which century did Cyrano de Bergerac live?

Answers to page 141
QUIZ 140: **1.** Ewan McGregor **2.** Michael Owen **3.** Fish **4.** A fear of chins **5.** France **6.** Quintin Hogg **7.** Crow **8.** Phil Daniels **9.** Ferdinand Magellan **10.** Richard Gere **11.** 9,000 **12.** Blue, black and white **13.** Table tennis **14.** A bat **15.** Paula Radcliffe **16.** Paul Gauguin

Quiz 139

Answers on page 138

1. What breed of bird led zoo keepers a merry dance in Norfolk in 2001?

2. Who was executed for the Oklahoma City bombing?

3. Which state capital of Delaware shares its name with a Kentish port?

4. Which Spice Girl recorded 'When You're Gone' with Bryan Adams?

5. Which liberalising Czechoslovak leader was arrested by Soviet troops during the 1968 invasion and subsequently expelled from the Communist Party?

6. Adam Gilchrist is a Test cricketer for which country?

7. Which river flows through the towns of Chatham, Gillingham and Rochester?

8. What do Murray Walker, Elizabeth Taylor and Jimmy Young have in common?

9. Which Hollywood legend once said: 'I acted vulgar, Madonna IS vulgar'?

10. In which country is the town of Oudenaarde?

11. How many gold medals did Jesse Owens win at the 1936 Berlin Olympics?

12. Which *Emmerdale* headmistress was killed by a car in September 2001?

13. What nationality is the singer Joni Mitchell?

14. In which ocean is the island of Nauru?

15. According to Greek mythology, who opened her box of evils?

16. What is a pronghorn?

Answers to page 138
QUIZ 137: **1.** Piltdown man **2.** Boris Karloff **3.** Elephant **4.** Greece **5.** *Not So Much a Programme, More a Way of Life* **6.** Ernest Rutherford **7.** Winchester **8.** Professor Yaffle **9.** Khartoum **10.** Charles II **11.** Sitting Bull **12.** 'Desire' **13.** Roses **14.** Dynamite was first devised by Alfred Nobel **15.** Echidna **16.** Chile

Quiz 140

Answers on page 139

1. Who starred in *Trainspotting* and *A Life Less Ordinary*?

2. Which footballer scored a hat-trick for England against Germany in 2001?

3. What is singer Derek Dick otherwise known as?

4. What is geniophobia?

5. In which country is Strasbourg?

6. Which British politician became Lord Hailsham?

7. The jay is a member of which family of birds?

8. Which actor sang on Blur's 'Parklife' single?

9. Which Portuguese navigator discovered the Philippines in 1521, only to be killed by natives?

10. Who played Billy Flynn in the film version of *Chicago*?

11. To the nearest 100 miles, how far is Perth, Australia, from London?

12. Which three colours feature on the national flag of Estonia?

13. At which sport was actor Paul Shane a junior champion?

14. What is a noctule?

15. Who won the BBC Sports Personality of the Year Award in 2002?

16. Who painted *Women of Tahiti*?

Answers to page 139
QUIZ 138: **1.** Elly May **2.** A power cut **3.** 1964 **4.** Margery Allingham **5.** Procul Harum **6.** Beginner's All-purpose Symbolic Instruction Code **7.** Carp **8.** Spain **9.** Hugh Hefner **10.** Thomas Edison **11.** Steven Gerrard (against Paul Gerard) **12.** Al Gore **13.** Brandy **14.** Ulrika Jonsson **15.** Crystal Palace **16.** 17th

Quiz 141

Answers on page 144

1. Which country is immediately to the north of Belize?

2. What nationality were the band Golden Earring who had a Seventies hit with 'Radar Love'?

3. Which is the nearest Communist country to the United States?

4. What is the average duration of sexual intercourse for humans?

5. Who blink more – men or women?

6. Where is a shrimp's heart?

7. What were Cinderella's slippers originally made out of before the story was changed by a 17th-century translator?

8. What happened to Ronald Reagan's chimpanzee co-star the day before the premiere of *Bedtime for Bonzo*?

9. At which cricket ground do bowlers come in from the Radcliffe Road end?

10. Who was Warren's despatch rider lover on *This Life*?

11. What are auctioned at Tattersalls?

12. Which member of the royal family joined the navy in 1971?

13. Lauryn Hill was singer with which nineties band?

14. What materials did the three little pigs use to build their houses?

15. What was Stephanie Rahn's claim to fame in 1970?

16. What creature is sometimes called an eft?

Answers to page 144
QUIZ 143: **1.** *The Adventures of Tom Sawyer* **2.** Sheffield **3.** A fruit **4.** Fulham **5.** Steven **6.** Austria **7.** Fiona Bruce **8.** New Guinea **9.** The Bodyline series **10.** 1997 **11.** New Mexico **12.** Spain **13.** Doris Day **14.** Canberra **15.** Harold Abrahams **16.** Julius Caesar

Quiz 142

Answers on page 145

1. Who scored a hat-trick in the Matthews' Cup Final?

2. Who starred in *Roxanne* and *My Blue Heaven*?

3. Which were the first Olympic Games to be televised live in Britain?

4. Which is the most easterly state in the USA?

5. Which English town is famous for its crooked spire?

6. In which county is the Prime Minister's country home, Chequers?

7. Who had a number one album in 2001 with *A Funk Odyssey*?

8. Where does a cow have its sweat glands?

9. At what age can a female lemming first become pregnant?

10. Who invented the motorists' aid, the cat's eye?

11. Which Dorset town is also the name of a city on the South Island of New Zealand?

12. What went down on 15 April 1912?

13. Which seventies band were formed at Charterhouse School?

14. Who was the Roman god of the underworld?

15. Nuuk is the capital of which country?

16. Who wrote *Circle of Friends* and *The Glass Lake*?

Answers to page 145

QUIZ 144: **1.** Dick Advocaat **2.** In your eye **3.** Five **4.** Klondike and Yukon **5.** Ingrid Bergman **6.** Goat **7.** USA and Mexico **8.** Mr Hodges **9.** Mongooses **10.** Sunday **11.** Hampshire **12.** The movie *Space Jam* **13.** The Cranberries **14.** Red **15.** Scotland **16.** George

Quiz 143

Answers on page 142

1. Which novel by Mark Twain was the first to be written on a typewriter?

2. In which English city is the Meadowhall Shopping Centre?

3. What is a wampee?

4. For which football club did 1966 World Cup hero George Cohen play?

5. What is Morrissey's first name?

6. Tirol is a province of which country?

7. Which Fiona co-presents *Crimewatch UK*?

8. The Torres Strait separates which country from Australia?

9. The controversial 1932 Test series between the cricketers of Australia and England became known as which series?

10. In which year did the charity single 'Perfect Day' reach number one?

11. Which American state is known as the 'Land of Enchantment'?

12. General Franco was dictator of which country from 1939?

13. Which Hollywood actress was nicknamed 'The Professional Virgin'?

14. The name of which Australian city means 'meeting-place'?

15. Which Olympic 100 metres champion was the subject of the film *Chariots of Fire*?

16. Who said: 'I came, I saw, I conquered'?

Answers to page 142
QUIZ 141: **1.** Mexico **2.** Dutch **3.** Cuba **4.** Two minutes **5.** Women **6.** In its head **7.** Fur **8.** It died **9.** Trent Bridge **10.** Ferdy **11.** Racehorses **12.** Prince Charles **13.** The Fugees **14.** Straw, sticks and bricks **15.** She was the first topless newspaper pin-up **16.** Newt

Quiz 144

Answers on page 143

1. Which Dutchman managed Rangers Football Club in 2001–2?

2. Where would you find vitreous humour?

3. How old was Arran Fernandez when he sat a maths GCSE examination in 2001?

4. The Canadian city of Dawson lies at the confluence of which two rivers?

5. Which Swedish actress starred in *Casablanca*?

6. Saanen, Hongtong and Toggenburg are all breeds of which animal?

7. Which two countries are separated by the Rio Grande?

8. What was the name of the officious ARP warden in *Dad's Army*?

9. What is the plural of mongoose?

10. On what day of the week must a month start in order for there to be a Friday the 13th?

11. Hayling Island is part of which English county?

12. What brought Bugs Bunny and basketball star Michael Jordan together in 1996?

13. Dolores O'Riordan is the singer with which band?

14. What is the principal colour of the Moroccan flag?

15. The thistle is the emblem of which country?

16. What was Babe Ruth's real Christian name?

Answers to page 143

QUIZ 142: **1.** Stan Mortensen **2.** Steve Martin **3.** The 1948 Olympics **4.** Maine **5.** Chesterfield **6.** Buckinghamshire **7.** Jamiroquai **8.** In its nose **9.** 14 days old **10.** Percy Shaw **11.** Christchurch **12.** The *Titanic* **13.** Genesis **14.** Pluto **15.** Greenland **16.** Maeve Binchy

Quiz 145

Answers on page 148

1. How high is the net in a game of table tennis?

2. Who played the Duke of Edinburgh as a cowardly swine on TV in 1983?

3. Which band was fronted by David Byrne?

4. Tahiti is the largest of which group of islands?

5. What was the name of the shaggy, piano-playing dog in *The Muppet Show*?

6. In which year did Bob Marley release 'No Woman No Cry'?

7. On which island is Margate?

8. What was the title of James Mason's final film?

9. Which judge looks after the baps?

10. What is the name of the chalk hill figure on the South Downs at Wilmington?

11. Which radio show featured Min and Henry Crun?

12. Which primrose opens at night?

13. Who won the 1995 Booker Prize with *The Ghost Road*?

14. What are roller, roman and venetian?

15. Which English explorer had the middle name Falcon?

16. Which river forms the eastern border between England and Scotland?

Answers to page 148
QUIZ 147: **1.** Arum lily **2.** Very low temperatures **3.** Cuckoo **4.** 12th **5.** Football **6.** Adam Adamant **7.** Salisbury Plain **8.** Germany **9.** Lord Lucan **10.** Peckham **11.** Philip Larkin **12.** Hale-Bopp comet **13.** *Romeo And Juliet* **14.** Spam **15.** *Spitting Image* **16.** A lemur-like creature

Quiz 146

Answers on page 149

1. How many days of Christmas are there?

2. What was the surname of the Bros boys?

3. What can be a ballet dancer's skirt or the name of a South African cleric?

4. What was the pen name of author Samuel Langhorne Clemens?

5. Which policy of Mikhail Gorbachev meant literally 'reconstruction'?

6. As what was Percy Toplis better known?

7. What is the capital of the Congo?

8. Which poet did Elizabeth Barrett marry?

9. What sporting activity takes place at Fairyhouse?

10. Which company was formed by Charlie Chaplin, Mary Pickford, Douglas Fairbanks and D. W. Griffith to distribute their films?

11. What is gneiss?

12. Who did the All Blacks play in a *Monty Python* rugby sketch?

13. Which English town houses the government surveillance centre, GCHQ?

14. Which boxer told his wife after losing his world heavyweight title in 1926: 'Honey, I just forgot to duck'?

15. Which French actor starred in the 1990 movie *Green Card*?

16. Which American state is known as the Centennial State?

Answers to page 149
QUIZ 148: **1.** Government Communications Headquarters **2.** *King Kong* **3.** Japan **4.** Axminster and Wilton **5.** Chris Langham **6.** January **7.** George III **8.** Glenn Close **9.** *Family Affairs* **10.** Federation Cup **11.** Terence **12.** Aries **13.** A type of tree **14.** Cerberus **15.** Donald Bradman **16.** Elton John (Roy Dwight)

Quiz 147

Answers on page 146

1. Which flower is also known as the calla lily?

2. What is cryogenics the science of?

3. What bird lays its eggs in the nests of other birds?

4. In which century did Saladin conquer Egypt?

5. What did George Bernard Shaw say was the only sport more boring than cricket?

6. Which TV superhero was played by Gerald Harper?

7. Westbury Down is the highest point of which stretch of English landscape?

8. The Ruhr Valley is a region of which country?

9. Whose car was found in Newhaven following his disappearance?

10. In which part of London did Del Boy and Rodney live?

11. Who wrote the 1964 poetry collection *The Whitsun Weddings*?

12. Which comet was discovered in 1995 by two American astronomers?

13. Which Shakespeare play was the title of a Dire Straits song?

14. Which tinned meat celebrated its 50th birthday in 1987?

15. Which TV show was created by Peter Fluck and Roger Law?

16. What is an aye-aye?

Answers to page 146
QUIZ 145: **1.** Six inches **2.** Rowan Atkinson (the first Edmund Blackadder's title was Duke of Edinburgh) **3.** Talking Heads **4.** Society Islands **5.** Rowlf **6.** 1974 **7.** Isle of Thanet **8.** *The Shooting Party* **9.** Master of the Rolls **10.** The 'Long Man' **11.** *The Goon Show* **12.** Evening primrose **13.** Pat Barker **14.** Types of window blind **15.** Captain Scott **16.** Tweed

Quiz 148

Answers on page 147

1. What does GCHQ stand for?

2. What was said to be Hitler's favourite film?

3. In which country might you be entertained by a geisha?

4. Which two English towns give their names to types of carpet?

5. Whom did Griff Rhys Jones replace in the *Not the Nine O'Clock News* team?

6. In which month does the Monte Carlo Rally traditionally take place?

7. In the reign of which King of England were the American colonies lost?

8. Who played the embittered mistress in *Fatal Attraction*?

9. Pete Callan is the resident villain in which TV soap?

10. In tennis, what is the women's equivalent of the Davis Cup?

11. What was Spike Milligan's real first name?

12. What is the first sign of the zodiac?

13. What is the bottlebrush?

14. In Greek mythology, what was the name of the three-headed dog guarding the entrance to the underworld?

15. Which Australian cricketer had a batting average of 99.94 from 52 Test matches?

16. Which singer had a cousin who scored an FA Cup final goal?

Answers to page 147
QUIZ 146: **1.** 12 **2.** Goss **3.** Tutu **4.** Mark Twain **5.** Perestroika **6.** 'The Monocled Mutineer'
7. Brazzaville **8.** Robert Browning **9.** Horse racing **10.** United Artists **11.** A type of rock **12.** Derby City Council **13.** Cheltenham **14.** Jack Dempsey **15.** Gérard Depardieu **16.** Colorado

Quiz 149

Answers on page 152

1. Which jockey won all seven races on the card at Ascot in 1996?

2. With which style of music is Scott Joplin associated?

3. How many points is the green ball worth in snooker?

4. In which county is Carlyon Bay where Tony Blair and his family went on holiday in 2001?

5. Which animal symbolises the zodiac sign Capricorn?

6. Which Swedish novelist was the first woman to win the Nobel Prize for Literature?

7. What nationality are rock band The Cardigans?

8. What is the name of *Frasier*'s father?

9. Which country inflicted Sven Goran Eriksson's first defeat as England football manager?

10. In which city was actress Angela Lansbury born?

11. Who was Britain's first Labour Prime Minister?

12. What is a prickly pear?

13. Where is Prince William Sound?

14. What were Vince and Penny in John Sullivan's sitcom?

15. Who wrote *The Railway Children*?

16. What are the names of Thomas the Tank Engine's two carriages?

Answers to page 152

QUIZ 151: **1.** Species of toad **2.** 16 **3.** Lambeth Bridge **4.** Flying **5.** Julio Iglesias **6.** Deep Blue Something **7.** South Wales **8.** Delft **9.** Anthony Hopkins **10.** Dennis Potter **11.** Kirk Douglas **12.** Douglas **13.** Coypu **14.** Great Bear **15.** Breed of pig **16.** Aldous Huxley

Quiz 150

Answers on page 153

1. In *Coronation Street*, which Battersby daughter was briefly married to Nick Tilsley?

2. Which heavy metal band took a ride on a 'Silver Machine'?

3. Which English city was called Glevum by the Romans?

4. Who won the Academy Award for Best Actor in 1996 for the film *Shine*?

5. In cricket, is the fielding position of extra cover situated on the off or the on side of the wicket?

6. Which is the smallest but most densely populated Central American country?

7. Ray Alan put words into the mouth of which mischievous schoolboy?

8. What type of bird is a pintail?

9. In which city would you find the Clifton Suspension Bridge?

10. Which wild flower has the Latin name *Digitalis*?

11. What does the fourth estate refer to?

12. Who succeeded Stephen as King of England in 1154?

13. What was Buddy Holly's real Christian name?

14. In which country does the Indus river rise?

15. What nationality is athlete Eunice Barber?

16. With which sport is Dennis Rodman associated?

Answers to page 153
QUIZ 152: **1.** Jacobite **2.** *Brookside* (an actor named Vincent Price played Jason Shadwick) **3.** German **4.** 'Seven Seas of Rhye' **5.** Bulgaria **6.** Albania **7.** Mel Blanc **8.** Cyprus **9.** A small antelope **10.** Rugby union **11.** Kojak **12.** Clement Attlee **13.** Spain **14.** Medical **15.** Potato **16.** Czech Republic

Quiz 151

Answers on page 150

1. What is a natterjack?

2. How many Popes have been called Gregory?

3. Heading west, what is the next London bridge after Westminster Bridge?

4. What is footballer Dennis Bergkamp afraid of?

5. Which singer used to be the goalkeeper for Real Madrid's reserve team?

6. Which band had a number one hit in 1996 with 'Breakfast at Tiffany's'?

7. Where are the Mumbles?

8. Which town in the Netherlands is famous for its pottery and porcelain?

9. Who starred in *Remains of the Day* and *Shadowlands*?

10. Which playwright's last TV dramas were *Karaoke* and *Cold Lazarus*?

11. Which actor was born Issur Danielovitch Demsky?

12. What is the capital of the Isle of Man?

13. Nutria is the fur of which animal?

14. What is the popular name for the constellation Ursa Major?

15. What is a Gloucester Old Spot?

16. Who wrote the science fiction novel *Brave New World*?

Answers to page 150
QUIZ 149: **1.** Frankie Dettori **2.** Ragtime **3.** Three **4.** Cornwall **5.** Goat **6.** Selma Lagerlof **7.** Swedish **8.** Martin **9.** Holland **10.** London **11.** Ramsay MacDonald **12.** Cactus **13.** The Gulf of Alaska **14.** *Just Good Friends* **15.** E. Nesbit **16.** Annie and Clarabel

Quiz 152

Answers on page 151

1. Which uprising led to the Battle of Killiecrankie in 1689?

2. Vincent Price has appeared in which British soap?

3. What nationality was St Bruno?

4. What was the title of Queen's first hit?

5. Sofia is the capital of which European country?

6. Who did England's footballers beat in another World Cup qualifier four days after trouncing Germany in September 2001?

7. Who provided the voice of Bugs Bunny but was allergic to carrots?

8. Larnaca and Kyrenia are ports on which island?

9. What is a dik-dik?

10. At which sport did Gareth Edwards excel for Wales?

11. Whose catchphrase was 'Who loves ya, baby'?

12. Who succeeded Winston Churchill as British Prime Minister in 1945?

13. In which country is Cape Finisterre?

14. Which profession takes the Hippocratic Oath?

15. The Colorado Beetle preys on which plant in particular?

16. Which country were world ice hockey champions in 1999 and 2000?

Answers to page 151
QUIZ 150: **1.** Leanne **2.** Hawkwind **3.** Gloucester **4.** Geoffrey Rush **5.** Off **6.** El Salvador **7.** Tich **8.** Duck **9.** Bristol **10.** Foxglove **11.** The press **12.** Henry II **13.** Charles **14.** Tibet **15.** French **16.** Basketball

Quiz 153

Answers on page 156

1. Which continent was explored by English navigator Matthew Flinders?

2. What nationality was the jeweller Fabergé?

3. Who invented the Kodak box camera?

4. Who was the first woman to fly across the Atlantic?

5. Which Hindu festival means 'garland of lamps'?

6. A dab is a member of which family of fish?

7. Which city is located at the western end of Hadrian's Wall?

8. Which fashion designer created the 'Space Age Collection' in the 1960s?

9. Who holds the record for the most tries scored in international rugby?

10. What type of insect does *Buddleia davidi* attract?

11. Who played the king in *The King and I*?

12. In which Australian state is the town of Ballarat?

13. What is an auricula?

14. Who wrote 'Auld Lang Syne'?

15. In 1960s music what were Unit Four Plus?

16. Which celebrated cook was born Isabella Mary Mayson?

Answers to page 156
QUIZ 155: **1.** Isle of Dogs **2.** Cassius Clay **3.** English Civil War **4.** El Cid **5.** A cheese **6.** Cheviot **7.** Walter Winterbottom **8.** Mason-Dixon Line **9.** Francisco Pizarro **10.** Massif Central **11.** Glottis **12.** Globe Theatre **13.** Tito Gobbi **14.** Marie Lloyd **15.** Geoffrey Durham **16.** Egypt

Quiz 154

Answers on page 157

1. The cane toad was introduced into Australia to eradicate which creature?

2. Fredericton is the capital of which Canadian province?

3. Which famous footballer was uncle to Jack and Bobby Charlton?

4. Which band recorded the album *Together Alone*?

5. In music, what is the term for a group of three or more notes sounded together?

6. In Greek mythology, which nymph was changed into a laurel tree?

7. Which tunnel, built in 1963, runs under the River Thames to Purfleet?

8. What does 'duce' mean in Italian?

9. What is a duiker?

10. Which US actress made her first starring appearance in the movie *Bonnie and Clyde* and later won an Oscar for *Network*?

11. In which country is the Curragh racecourse?

12. What can be gold, green or zebra?

13. Rustavi and Batumi are towns in which country?

14. Who won his first Formula One Grand Prix in Hungary in 1993?

15. In which country is the Lena river?

16. Which British tennis star's wife had a baby girl named Rose in October 2002?

Answers to page 157
QUIZ 156: **1.** *Mona Lisa* **2.** Perry **3.** Joe DiMaggio **4.** Mock Orange **5.** Way of living **6.** Ed Moses **7.** Bob Marley **8.** Conchita Martínez **9.** France **10.** Izaak Walton **11.** Type of deer **12.** Witham **13.** Swift **14.** Broom **15.** Compact Disc Read-Only Memory **16.** The Chair

Quiz 155

Answers on page 154

1. On which island is Canary Wharf?

2. Who changed his name to Muhammad Ali?

3. Edgehill was the opening battle in which war?

4. What was the nickname of Spanish soldier Rodrigo Díaz de Vivar?

5. What is Cucciocavallo?

6. Which range of hills in Northumberland gave their name to a breed of sheep?

7. Who preceded Alf Ramsey as England football manager?

8. What is the name of the boundary line between Maryland and Pennsylvania?

9. Which Spanish conquistador conquered Peru?

10. What is the mountainous plateau region of southern central France?

11. What is the narrow opening at the upper end of the larynx that contains the vocal cords?

12. Which London theatre was burned down in 1613 after a fired cannon set light to the thatch during a performance of Shakespeare's *Henry VIII*?

13. Which Gobbi was an Italian baritone?

14. Which music-hall artist was born Matilda Alice Victoria Wood?

15. Which magician separated from Victoria Wood after more than 20 years of marriage?

16. Which country is immediately to the east of Libya?

Answers to page 154
QUIZ 153: **1.** Australia **2.** Russian **3.** George Eastman **4.** Amelia Earhart **5.** Diwali **6.** Flounder
7. Carlisle **8.** Pierre Cardin **9.** David Campese **10.** Butterflies **11.** Yul Brynner **12.** Victoria
13. A species of primrose **14.** Robert Burns **15.** Two **16.** Mrs Beeton

Quiz 156

Answers on page 155

1. Which painting is also known as *La Gioconda*?

2. Who is Kevin the teenager's best friend?

3. Which baseball star was Marilyn Monroe's second husband?

4. What sort of orange is a shrub with white scented flowers?

5. What does the Latin modus vivendi mean?

6. Which 400 metres hurdler went 122 races unbeaten from 1977 to 1987?

7. Who recorded the 1972 album *Catch a Fire*?

8. Who beat Martina Navratilova in the 1994 Wimbledon ladies' singles final?

9. In which country is the Var river?

10. Who wrote *The Compleat Angler*?

11. What is a wapiti?

12. On which river does the Lincolnshire town of Boston stand?

13. As in the breed of dog, what does the Russian word 'borzoi' mean?

14. What can be a flowering shrub or an implement for sweeping?

15. What does CD-ROM stand for?

16. What is the highest fence in the Grand National?

Answers to page 155
QUIZ 154: **1.** The cane beetle **2.** New Brunswick **3.** Jackie Milburn **4.** Crowded House **5.** Chord **6.** Daphne **7.** Dartford Tunnel **8.** Leader **9.** A small antelope **10.** Faye Dunaway **11.** Ireland **12.** Finches **13.** Georgia **14.** Damon Hill **15.** Russia **16.** Tim Henman

— 157 —

Quiz 157

Answers on page 160

1. Which English city had the Roman name 'Aquae Sulis'?

2. Which 11-year-old qualified for the National Chess Championships in 1977?

3. Which European country held its first democratic election for 41 years in June 1977?

4. What was the name of Regan and Carter's boss in *The Sweeney*?

5. Which US sitcom star provided the voice of Sideshow Bob on *The Simpsons*?

6. Who said: 'I think for the life span he's lasted, Chuck Berry's productivity has been nil, more or less'?

7. Who was the first British footballer to be paid £100 a week?

8. What is 15 squared?

9. Why were parts of Britain temporarily plunged into darkness on 11 August 1999?

10. Gomera and Hierro are part of which group of islands?

11. How many hours are New Zealand ahead of Britain?

12. What colour are the flowers of the dogwood?

13. What animal lives in a lodge?

14. Which mountain did Horace Saussure make the first ascent of in 1787?

15. William the Silent was the ruler of which country from 1572 to 1584?

16. Who gave thanks for the Aintree Iron?

Answers to page 160
QUIZ 159: **1.** Lincoln City **2.** Edwina Currie **3.** They were all once librarians **4.** The Prince Regent
5. Contact lens **6.** Bob Carolgees **7.** David Gray **8.** Shipping areas **9.** Mark Knopfler (Dire Straits)
10. *Shakespeare in Love* **11.** It was the first dog in space **12.** Algeria **13.** Mike Tyson **14.** Ian Smith
15. Suffolk **16.** Argentine

Quiz 158

Answers on page 161

1. Who sang about 'Sunshine on a Rainy Day' in 1991?

2. Under which pseudonym did French architect Charles Edouard Jeanneret work?

3. In which city were the 1996 Olympics held?

4. Who discovered the mouth of the River Amazon in 1499?

5. Barbara Windsor succeeded Jo Warne in which role?

6. What is Bono's real name?

7. Which actor's contract with MGM in the 1920s forbade him from smiling on screen?

8. The Maledicta Society caters for people who like to do what?

9. Who directed *Gregory's Girl*?

10. In which year did Concorde make its first flight?

11. The Dalai Lama is the spiritual head of which country?

12. What is the nickname of Leicester's rugby team?

13. On which river does Derby stand?

14. Who wrote the spy thriller *The Ipcress File*?

15. Who was the first golfer to win two successive US Masters titles?

16. What was the Christian name of the English scientist Faraday?

Answers to page 161
QUIZ 160: **1.** A tittle **2.** Ag **3.** Vladimir Putin **4.** 'The Ballad of John and Yoko' **5.** Charles I **6.** Daisy **7.** Yellow **8.** Sunshine Desserts **9.** Chlorophyll **10.** Dodecanese **11.** Elizabeth I **12.** Baseball **13.** 17th **14.** *Twelfth Night* **15.** Thomas Hearns **16.** Grampians

Quiz 159

Answers on page 158

1. Which was the first Football League club to be relegated to the Conference?

2. Which junior health minister resigned in 1988 following a row about the presence of salmonella in eggs?

3. What did Mao Tse-Tung, Casanova and Anthea Turner have in common?

4. Who ordered the building of the Royal Pavilion in Brighton?

5. Which optical aid was invented by the German Adolph E. Fick in 1887?

6. Who has a dog named Spit?

7. Who released the album *White Ladder*?

8. What are Dogger, Fastnet and German Bight?

9. Which leader of a popular eighties band has the middle name Freuder?

10. Which Guy Madden movie won an Oscar for Best Film in 1998?

11. What was Laika's claim to fame in the story of space travel?

12. In which country was the writer Albert Camus born?

13. In 1986, which boxer became the youngest World Heavyweight Champion?

14. Which Rhodesian leader declared his country's unilateral independence from Britain in 1965?

15. In which county is Bury St Edmunds?

16. What nationality is tennis player Gabriela Sabatini?

Answers to page 158
QUIZ 157: **1.** Bath **2.** Nigel Short **3.** Spain **4.** Frank Haskins **5.** Kelsey Grammer **6.** Sir Elton John **7.** Johnny Haynes **8.** 225 **9.** Total solar eclipse **10.** Canary Islands **11.** 12 **12.** White **13.** Beaver **14.** Mont Blanc **15.** The Netherlands **16.** Scaffold

Quiz 160

Answers on page 159

1. What is the name for the dot over the letter 'i'?

2. What is the chemical symbol for silver?

3. Who succeeded Boris Yeltsin as Russian President?

4. What was The Beatles' last UK number one single?

5. Which English king was beheaded in 1649?

6. *Bellis perennis* is more commonly known as which wild flower?

7. What colour jersey is worn by the leader in the Tour de France cycle race?

8. For which food manufacturing company did Reggie Perrin work?

9. What is the name of the green pigment that is present in most plants?

10. Rhodes and Kos are part of which group of islands?

11. To whom was the poem *The Faerie Queene* dedicated?

12. What sport do the Atlanta Braves play?

13. In which century did the dodo become extinct?

14. Sir Toby Belch and Sir Andrew Aguecheek are characters in which Shakespeare play?

15. In 1988 which American became the first boxer to win world titles at five different weight classes in five separate fights?

16. Which range of mountains separates the Highlands and Lowlands of Scotland?

Answers to page 159
QUIZ 158: **1.** Zoe **2.** Le Corbusier **3.** Atlanta **4.** Amerigo Vespucci **5.** *EastEnders'* Peggy Mitchell
6. Paul Hewson **7.** Buster Keaton **8.** Swear **9.** Bill Forsyth **10.** 1969 **11.** Tibet **12.** Tigers
13. Derwent **14.** Len Deighton **15.** Jack Nicklaus **16.** Michael

Quiz 161

Answers on page 164

1. The first pair of what brand of boots were made from tyres?

2. What is the capital of Chile?

3. Which insect can spend over a year in its larval stage yet only lives for a day as an adult?

4. Approximately how many species of bat are there – 500, 800, 1,000?

5. Where on the human body is the femur?

6. The Bessemer process was the first economical method of making which product?

7. Which card game originated in 1925 on a steamer travelling from Los Angeles to Havana?

8. In which country is the town of Coober Pedy?

9. In which county is Blenheim Palace?

10. Which city will stage the 2006 Commonwealth Games?

11. In which year was the breathalyser first introduced to the UK?

12. Which TV show was first broadcast on New Year's Day 1964 from a converted Manchester church?

13. Tony Hadley was the lead singer with which eighties band?

14. Who was found dead in the opening episode of *EastEnders*?

15. What nationality was the Renaissance scholar Erasmus?

16. Who broke Pete Sampras's run of Wimbledon tennis victories by winning the 1996 men's singles title?

Answers to page 164
QUIZ 163: **1.** Giacomo Agostini **2.** Carmen Miranda **3.** Herring **4.** Eric Morecambe **5.** Yellow **6.** 17th
7. Augusta **8.** Sir Christopher Wren **9.** Harriet Beecher Stowe **10.** Anita Ward **11.** Everton
12. Benton Fraser (*Due South*): dog Diefenbaker **13.** Escalator **14.** John Lennon **15.** Honduras
16. The Jockey Club

Quiz 162

Answers on page 165

1. Which astronaut's mother's maiden name was Moon?

2. Which country has a town called A?

3. In the TV series, which *Batman* villain was played by Cesar Romero?

4. For which county cricket team did David Gower play from 1975 to 1989?

5. Who was the god of wine in Roman mythology?

6. How many players are there in a women's lacrosse team?

7. Who composed 'The Entertainer', used as the theme tune for the film *The Sting*?

8. What is a joule?

9. Who won the Men's World Squash Championships six times in the 1980s?

10. Which battle took place south of Calais on 25 October 1415?

11. Where is the administrative centre of Cornwall?

12. What does the CIA stand for?

13. Who was the baker in *Camberwick Green*?

14. Which Hollywood actress was born Shirley Schrift before borrowing part of her new name from a poet?

15. What is a dhole?

16. In which American state is Las Vegas?

Answers to page 165
QUIZ 164: **1.** 1955 **2.** T'Pau **3.** Essex **4.** Wear **5.** Kingcup **6.** Kent **7.** Sir Robert Walpole **8.** Three **9.** The Peninsular War **10.** Henry VII **11.** Bob Beamon **12.** Tom Watson **13.** Scotland **14.** California **15.** Mount McKinley **16.** Stockholm

Quiz 163

Answers on page 162

1. Which Italian motorcyclist won a record 122 Grands Prix and 15 world titles?

2. Which Hollywood actress was nicknamed 'The Brazilian Bombshell'?

3. Which is the world's most widely eaten fish?

4. In 1995 a carving of John Smith was removed from Labour Party HQ when passers-by mistook it for a statue of which comedian?

5. What colour are the flowers of agrimony?

6. In which century did the Baroque style dominate European art?

7. What is the state capital of Maine?

8. Which architect designed the Royal Greenwich Observatory?

9. Which American novelist wrote *Uncle Tom's Cabin*?

10. Whose only UK hit was the 1979 number one 'Ring My Bell'?

11. Who were the first British football club to install undersoil heating?

12. Which TV cop's dog was named after a former Canadian Prime Minister?

13. What did Jesse W. Reno invent in 1892?

14. Which Beatle sang backing vocals on David Bowie's 'Fame'?

15. Tegucigalpa is the capital of which Central American country?

16. What is the governing body of English horse racing?

Answers to page 162
QUIZ 161: **1.** Doc Martens **2.** Santiago **3.** Mayfly **4.** 1,000 **5.** The thigh **6.** Steel **7.** Contract bridge **8.** Australia **9.** Oxfordshire **10.** Melbourne **11.** 1967 **12.** *Top of the Pops* **13.** Spandau Ballet **14.** Reg Cox **15.** Dutch **16.** Richard Krajicek

Quiz 164

Answers on page 163

1. In which year did ITV start?

2. Which eighties band took their name from Mr Spock's Vulcan friend in *Star Trek*?

3. For which county did former England cricket captain Graham Gooch play?

4. On which river does Durham stand?

5. What is another name for the marsh marigold?

6. In which county is Leeds Castle?

7. Who was the first British Prime Minister?

8. How many hearts does an octopus have?

9. Salamanca and Vittoria were battles in which war?

10. Who was the first Tudor King of England?

11. Who won the long jump at the 1968 Mexico Olympics?

12. Which golfer won his fifth British Open in 1983?

13. Who was defeated at the Battle of Pinkie?

14. In which American state is the San Andreas fault?

15. Which is the highest mountain in North America?

16. In which city were the 1912 Olympic Games staged?

Answers to page 163
QUIZ 162: **1.** Buzz Aldrin **2.** Norway **3.** The Joker **4.** Leicestershire **5.** Bacchus **6.** 12 **7.** Scott Joplin **8.** A unit of work or energy **9.** Jahangir Khan **10.** Agincourt **11.** Truro **12.** Central Intelligence Agency **13.** Mickey Murphy **14.** Shelley Winters **15.** An Asian wild dog **16.** Nevada

Quiz 165

Answers on page 168

1. Which former England football manager was born on the same day as Yoko Ono – 18 February 1933?

2. Which American state is nicknamed the 'Wolverine State'?

3. Which French playwright died on stage while playing a hypochondriac in his own play *Le Malade Imaginaire*?

4. Which TV detective had the Christian name 'Endeavour'?

5. Which Poet Laureate once declared himself to be a huge fan of *Coronation Street*?

6. What was the first James Bond film?

7. What took place in Londonderry on 30 January 1972?

8. At the 1980 Olympics, who became the first Briton since Harold Abrahams to win the men's 100 metres?

9. Which acid is contained in vinegar?

10. Who was President of Ireland between 1959 and 1973?

11. Who was the Roman goddess of the Moon?

12. In which country is the Chihuahuan Desert?

13. What was the title of the US version of *Cracker*?

14. What is the golfing term for a score of three under par at a hole?

15. What was the name of the bridge in Buckinghamshire where the Great Train Robbery took place?

16. In which ship did the Pilgrim Fathers sail?

Answers to page 168
QUIZ 167: **1.** David Livermore (Millwall) **2.** Boston **3.** Stringed **4.** The leaves **5.** Elbe **6.** Thanksgiving **7.** Hugh Scully **8.** Edward G. Robinson **9.** Anton Chekhov **10.** All are qualified pilots **11.** Fender Broadcaster **12.** Thomas **13.** Milan **14.** Harold Macmillan **15.** The Police **16.** The watt (James Watt)

Quiz 166

Answers on page 169

1. Which Spice Girl was once an extra in *Emmerdale*?

2. Who played Fred Flintstone in the movie version of *The Flintstones*?

3. Which swimmer was the first woman to win the BBC Sports Personality of the Year Award?

4. Who was found dead in her bed on 5 August 1962?

5. Why were Donald Duck comics once banned in Finland?

6. What nationality was the composer Grieg?

7. Warkworth Castle is situated in which English county?

8. Sharleen Spiteri is the singer with which band?

9. What was sent to attack England in 1588?

10. Who retained the Formula One World Drivers' Championship in 2002?

11. What is the name given to the side opposite the right angle of a triangle?

12. The Phantom Flan Flinger wreaked havoc on which Saturday morning TV show?

13. Who wrote *King Solomon's Mines*?

14. Which football team are nicknamed the Baggies?

15. Which BBC reporter ousted Neil Hamilton as MP for Tatton at the 1997 general election?

16. Who stuck to his principles at the Diet of Worms?

Answers to page 169
QUIZ 168: **1.** Pope John Paul II **2.** Australia **3.** St Anne's **4.** Gerry and The Pacemakers **5.** Twiggy **6.** Creighton-Ward **7.** Gary Cooper **8.** George III **9.** All were born on Christmas Day **10.** Vincent Van Gogh **11.** Freddie Starr **12.** Verdi **13.** Julius **14.** Annapolis **15.** Hungary **16.** Sodor

Quiz 167

Answers on page 166

1. Which player scored the last Football League goal of the 20th century?

2. In which American city was *Cheers* set?

3. What kind of musical instrument is a lute?

4. What parts of the rhubarb plant are poisonous?

5. On which river is the city of Hamburg?

6. What national holiday do Americans celebrate on the fourth Thursday in November?

7. Who did Michael Aspel replace as presenter of *Antiques Roadshow*?

8. Which Hollywood tough guy of the 1930s was born Emanuel Goldenberg?

9. Who wrote *Uncle Vanya* and *The Three Sisters*?

10. What do John Travolta, Gary Numan and Nicholas Lyndhurst have in common?

11. What was the first solid-body electric guitar?

12. What was the Christian name of the English landscape painter Gainsborough?

13. Which horse – bearing the name of an Italian city – won the 2001 St Leger?

14. Which former British Prime Minister became the first Earl of Stockton?

15. Which band released the album *Reggatta de Blanc*?

16. Which unit of power is named after the Scottish engineer who developed early models of the steam engine?

Answers to page 166
QUIZ 165: **1.** Bobby Robson **2.** Michigan **3.** Molière **4.** Inspector Morse **5.** Sir John Betjeman **6.** *Dr No* **7.** Bloody Sunday **8.** Allan Wells **9.** Acetic acid **10.** Eamon de Valera **11.** Luna **12.** Mexico **13.** *Fitz* **14.** Albatross **15.** Bridego Bridge **16.** *Mayflower*

Quiz 168

Answers on page 167

1. Who was the most famous goalkeeper in the history of Polish amateur club Wotsyla?

2. The Gulf of Carpentaria lies off the coast of which country?

3. What is the capital of the Channel Island of Alderney?

4. Who were the first Merseybeat group to have a UK number one single?

5. Which model was named Woman of the Year for 1966?

6. What was Lady Penelope's surname in *Thunderbirds*?

7. Who turned down the role of Rhett Butler in *Gone With the Wind* because he was convinced it would be a flop?

8. Who was the longest reigning King of England?

9. What do Sir Isaac Newton, Kenny Everett and Annie Lennox have in common?

10. Who was sacked from his job as assistant to a Paris art dealer for sneaking off to Holland at Christmas and for being rude to customers?

11. Which comedian owned the 1994 Grand National winner, Minnehoma?

12. Who composed the operas *Rigoletto* and *La Traviata*?

13. What was Groucho Marx's real name?

14. What is the state capital of Maryland?

15. The forint is the standard currency of which country?

16. On which fictitious island does *Thomas the Tank Engine* operate?

Answers to page 167
QUIZ 166: **1.** Melanie Brown **2.** John Goodman **3.** Anita Lonsborough **4.** Marilyn Monroe **5.** Because he doesn't wear pants **6.** Norwegian **7.** Northumberland **8.** Texas **9.** Spanish Armada **10.** Michael Schumacher **11.** Hypotenuse **12.** *Tiswas* **13.** Rider Haggard **14.** West Bromwich Albion **15.** Martin Bell **16.** Martin Luther

Quiz 169

Answers on page 172

1. In which county is Beamish open-air industrial museum?

2. Who rode Shergar to victory in the Epsom Derby?

3. Which city is the administrative headquarters of Tayside?

4. Who recorded 'Earth Song'?

5. What nationality is tennis player Ivan Lendl?

6. Which creatures sometimes hurl themselves to their deaths over cliffs during mass migrations?

7. Who are the team captains on *Never Mind the Buzzcocks*?

8. What is the first day of Lent?

9. Who starred in *Hudson Hawk* and *The Last Boy Scout*?

10. What is the state capital of New Mexico?

11. According to the Irish proverb, what do bare walls make?

12. What is nephelophobia?

13. Which model starred in the film *The Boyfriend*?

14. The quetzal is the currency of which country?

15. In Greek mythology, who was the mother of Artemis and Apollo?

16. David Bryant was an English champion at which sport?

Answers to page 172
QUIZ 171: **1.** *Harry Potter and the Order of the Phoenix* **2.** Quentin Crisp **3.** John Surtees **4.** 1,001
5. Tawe **6.** Society Islands **7.** Tennis **8.** Libra, Aquarius and Gemini **9.** Cormorant **10.** 4 July
11. Desert Orchid **12.** March and September **13.** Tagus **14.** Charles II **15.** Afghanistan
16. *Bright Eyes*

Quiz 170

Answers on page 173

1. Which playing card was a hit with Motörhead?

2. What string of beads is used in a Catholic prayer?

3. *Salvia officianalis* is better known as which herb?

4. Who was Noggin the Nog's wicked uncle?

5. Where do barnacles have their ovaries?

6. In 1984, who called the National Gallery extension a 'monstrous carbuncle'?

7. Which human organ contains the smallest bones?

8. By what colour is the District Line depicted on London Underground maps?

9. Sir Walter Tyrrel inadvertently killed which English king?

10. Which Hollywood entertainer was born Frederick Austerlitz?

11. Who was appointed Poet Laureate in 1968?

12. What does 'scherzo' mean in music?

13. Where is Cape Wrath?

14. Which controversial product went on sale in Britain for the first time in 1961 although it was not available on prescription for another two years?

15. What nationality is tennis player Martina Hingis?

16. Which London mayor introduced the Congestion Charge?

Answers to page 173
QUIZ 172: **1.** Lord Byron **2.** *Mansfield Park* **3.** Blue **4.** Pretenders to the throne in the reign of Henry VII **5.** Albania and Italy **6.** Ostrich **7.** The Jam **8.** Trevor Jordache **9.** Joan Crawford **10.** Addis Ababa **11.** Jack Taylor **12.** James **13.** Dopey **14.** On a tennis court **15.** Terrier **16.** Long John Silver's

Quiz 171

Answers on page 170

1. What is the title of the fifth book in the Harry Potter series?

2. Who was the subject of Sting's song 'An Englishman in New York'?

3. Who is the only person to have won world titles on two and four wheels?

4. How many nights are there in the *Arabian Nights*?

5. Swansea is situated at the mouth of which river?

6. Tahiti is the largest of which group of islands?

7. At which sport do countries compete for the Davis Cup?

8. What are the three air signs of the zodiac?

9. A shag is a small species of which seabird?

10. What date is Independence Day in the USA?

11. Which racehorse was affectionately known as 'Dessie'?

12. Which two months have equinoxes?

13. Which river rises in Aragon, Spain, and reaches the Atlantic at Lisbon, Portugal?

14. Orange-seller Nell Gwynn was a mistress of which English monarch?

15. Which country forms the southern border of Tajikistan?

16. In which film did Shirley Temple sing 'On the Good Ship Lollipop'?

Answers to page 170
QUIZ 169: **1.** Durham **2.** Walter Swinburn **3.** Dundee **4.** Michael Jackson **5.** Czech **6.** Lemmings **7.** Bill Bailey and Phill Jupitus **8.** Ash Wednesday **9.** Bruce Willis **10.** Santa Fe **11.** Giddy housekeepers **12.** Fear of clouds **13.** Twiggy **14.** Guatemala **15.** Leto **16.** Bowls

Quiz 172

Answers on page 171

1. Which poet kept a pet bear at Cambridge University because dogs weren't allowed?

2. Fanny Price was a character in which Jane Austen novel?

3. What colour is a lobster's blood?

4. Who were Lambert Simnel and Perkin Warbeck?

5. The Strait of Otranto separates which two countries?

6. What bird lays the largest egg?

7. Who sang about a 'Town Called Malice'?

8. Who was buried under the patio of 10 Brookside Close?

9. Which actress called Elizabeth Taylor 'a spoiled, indulgent child, a blemish on public decency'?

10. The name of which capital city means 'new flower'?

11. Which British referee awarded a penalty inside the first minute of the 1974 World Cup Final?

12. Tim Booth is the singer with which band?

13. Which is the only one of the Seven Dwarfs without a beard?

14. Where would you find tramlines on grass?

15. Cairn, Sealyham and Bedlington are all types of what?

16. Whose shoulder did Captain Flint perch on?

Answers to page 171
QUIZ 170: **1.** 'Ace Of Spades' **2.** Rosary **3.** Sage **4.** Nogbad the Bad **5.** In their heads **6.** Prince Charles **7.** The ear **8.** Green **9.** William Rufus **10.** Fred Astaire **11.** Cecil Day-Lewis **12.** Lively **13.** Scotland **14.** The Pill **15.** Swiss **16.** Ken Livingstone

Quiz 173

Answers on page 176

1. Which daughter of a former *Blue Peter* presenter sang on a number one hit in 2000?

2. In Greek mythology, which beautiful youth was the favourite of the goddess Aphrodite?

3. Which cord connects a foetus to the placenta?

4. What colour is the lignite jet?

5. Which TV inquisitor described herself as an 'ageing ex-drunk with bad ankles'?

6. How many world championship points are awarded to the driver who comes second in a Formula One Grand Prix?

7. Where on your body might you wear puttees?

8. Which Spice Girl teamed up with Truesteppers and Dane Bowers for the 2000 single 'Out of Your Mind'?

9. Who was known as 'The Virgin Queen'?

10. What is the cube of four?

11. Who wrote the fantasy novel *The Colour of Magic*?

12. Which English actor played law firm boss Ed Masry in the movie *Erin Brockovich*?

13. The US city of Cleveland is on the shores of which Great Lake?

14. Which two colours feature in the Spanish national flag?

15. In which sport did teams contest the Regal Trophy between 1971 and 1996?

16. The Amazon flows into the sea in which country?

Answers to page 176
QUIZ 175: **1.** Victoria Beckham (Brooklyn) **2.** Icarus **3.** Michelle Pfeiffer **4.** Antarctica **5.** New South Wales **6.** 1968 **7.** Berkshire **8.** Bowls **9.** Father Peter Clifford **10.** Kenny Dalglish **11.** Seven **12.** Dock **13.** Lord Grade **14.** Double vision **15.** Duke of Windsor **16.** Thomas Hardy

Quiz 174

Answers on page 177

1. What colour is given to the name of the room at studios where actors rest?

2. Who was the first Tory Prime Minister of Britain?

3. What is a native of Manchester called?

4. Bernadotte is the family name of which country's royal house?

5. Where would you find a Bezier curve?

6. Which Football League manager parted company with his club in September 2001 after nearly 12 years in charge?

7. Which Pakistan premier was the first female leader of a Muslim state?

8. What does BFI stand for?

9. The dace is a member of which family of freshwater fish?

10. Which sports presenter was the subject of an expensive transfer from BBC to ITV in 1999?

11. 'Peaches' was the first UK top ten hit for which punk rockers?

12. Which Jonathan Kaplan film earned Jodie Foster an Academy Award for Best Actress in 1988?

13. In which city do visitors land at Marco Polo Airport?

14. Which countries form the Iberian Peninsula?

15. Which singer made his big-screen debut in the film *8 Mile*?

16. Who romanced Renée Zellweger in the film *Jerry Maguire*?

Answers to page 177

QUIZ 176: **1.** 1923 **2.** Stephen Fry **3.** Six **4.** Mushroom **5.** Sash! **6.** Darts **7.** Switzerland **8.** Guns 'N' Roses **9.** Deadly nightshade **10.** Adolf Eichmann **11.** Greenland **12.** Suzanne Charlton **13.** Esperanto **14.** CD **15.** Newcastle-upon-Tyne **16.** Yerevan

— 175 —

Quiz 175

Answers on page 174

1. Which singer's baby son could be heard on her 2001 album?

2. In Greek mythology, who plunged to his death after flying too close to the Sun?

3. Who was 'Makin' Whoopee' in *The Fabulous Baker Boys*?

4. In which continent is the Weddell Sea?

5. The town of Newcastle is in which Australian state?

6. Before 2001, when was the last time that Fulham's footballers were in the top division?

7. In which county is Bracknell?

8. Which outdoor game is played on a grass area known as a rink?

9. What was the name of the priest played by Stephen Tompkinson in *Ballykissangel*?

10. Who was the first professional footballer to score 100 goals in both Scotland and England?

11. After how many games in a lawn tennis match are the players given new balls?

12. Which plant's leaves cure nettle stings?

13. Which TV chief said of his forthcoming production *Moses the Lawgiver*: 'It looks good in the rushes'?

14. What do you suffer from if you have diplopia?

15. What title was Edward VIII given following his abdication?

16. Which novelist revived the term 'Wessex' to describe the south-west counties of England?

Answers to page 174
QUIZ 173: **1.** Sophie Ellis Bextor (daughter of Janet Ellis) **2.** Adonis **3.** Umbilical cord **4.** Black **5.** Anne Robinson **6.** Six **7.** On your legs **8.** Victoria Beckham **9.** Elizabeth I **10.** 64 **11.** Terry Pratchett **12.** Albert Finney **13.** Lake Erie **14.** Red and yellow **15.** Rugby League **16.** Brazil

Quiz 176

Answers on page 175

1. In which year was Wembley Stadium first opened?

2. Who played the troubled playwright in the 1997 biopic of Oscar Wilde?

3. How many times has Steve Davis been World Snooker Champion?

4. The death cap is the most poisonous type of what?

5. Whose first UK hit was 'Encore Une Fois' in 1997?

6. Leighton Rees and Bobby George are practitioners of which sport?

7. Helvetia is another name for which country?

8. Slash is the guitarist with which heavy rock band?

9. Which plant's proper name is belladonna?

10. Which Nazi was executed after being tried in Israel in 1961 for war crimes?

11. Eric the Red is said to have been the first European to discover which land?

12. Which daughter of a famous footballer has been a weather forecaster for the BBC?

13. Which international language was devised by Ludwig L. Zamenhof?

14. What musical medium is 400 in Roman numerals?

15. In which English city is the district of Byker?

16. What is the capital of Armenia?

Answers to page 175
QUIZ 174: **1.** Green **2.** Earl of Bute **3.** Mancunian **4.** Sweden **5.** On a graph **6.** Brian Flynn (Wrexham) **7.** Benazir Bhutto **8.** British Film Institute **9.** Carp **10.** Des Lynam **11.** The Stranglers **12.** *The Accused* **13.** Venice **14.** Spain and Portugal **15.** Eminem **16.** Tom Cruise

Quiz 177

Answers on page 180

1. In which continent are the Atlas Mountains?

2. Which punk band were 'Turning Japanese' in 1980?

3. Which was the chosen event of British athlete Roger Black?

4. What colour were post boxes originally?

5. What form of transport was pioneered by Igor Sikorsky?

6. Which Russian novelist wrote *Crime and Punishment*?

7. What was Victoria Beckham's maiden name?

8. What product was Henry Doulton's speciality?

9. Jason Durr took over from Nick Berry in which TV series?

10. What did my true love give to me on the third day of Christmas?

11. As which sixties band were Scott Engel, John Maus and Gary Leeds better known?

12. For what is ENT an abbreviation in medicine?

13. Who makes 'exceedingly good cakes'?

14. In what form of theatre did Ben Travers specialise?

15. What is a fata morgana?

16. Which Hollywood comic was born Joseph Levitch?

Answers to page 180
QUIZ 179: **1.** *Rebecca* **2.** Côte d'Azur **3.** Fred Trueman **4.** Tom Cruise **5.** Butterflies **6.** Barney and Betty Rubble **7.** Constantinople **8.** Caspian Sea **9.** 'The' **10.** Amerigo Vespucci **11.** Steve Cauthen **12.** Dollar **13.** Llandudno **14.** A type of onion **15.** Indiana **16.** Concorde

Quiz 178

Answers on page 181

1. Some 60,000 men were killed on the first day of which First World War battle?

2. Which actor's middle name is Columcille?

3. What number on the Beaufort Scale indicates a gale?

4. Varna is a port on which sea?

5. Which James Bond once advertised Big Fry chocolate bars?

6. Who was the Greek goddess of the Earth?

7. Who wrote *The Darling Buds of May*?

8. Which Football League team are nicknamed the 'Chairboys'?

9. Which Post Office executive invented adhesive stamps in the 19th century?

10. In which year did the Easter Rising take place in Dublin?

11. Which band released the album *Automatic for the People*?

12. Rosencrantz and Guildenstern featured in which Shakespeare play?

13. Who painted *The Laughing Cavalier*?

14. Which English cricketer took a world record 19 wickets in a Test match against Australia in 1956?

15. The Barras is a market in which British city?

16. Who was Richie Rich's agent?

Answers to page 181
QUIZ 180: **1.** Dartmoor **2.** Cardiff **3.** Turin **4.** John Cleese **5.** Steven Spielberg **6.** *Riverdance* **7.** Arthur C. Clarke **8.** Canada **9.** Pluto **10.** 21% **11.** Australia **12.** Fatboy Slim **13.** Both were called Eric **14.** A joey **15.** Chester **16.** Japan

Quiz 179

Answers on page 178

1. Which novel was set in a house called Manderley?

2. What is the name for the stretch of coastline which connects St Tropez, Cannes and Nice?

3. In 1964, which English cricketer became the first bowler to take 300 Test wickets?

4. Which Hollywood star enrolled to become a priest at 14, but dropped out after a year?

5. What are red admirals and swallow tails?

6. Who adopted Bamm Bamm?

7. Which city was the capital of the Byzantine empire?

8. Astrakhan and Baku are the chief ports on which inland sea?

9. What is the most commonly used word in written English?

10. Which explorer gave his name to America?

11. Which American was UK champion jockey in 1984, 1985 and 1987?

12. Thereze Bazaar and David Van Day made up which singing duo?

13. The Great Orme is near which Welsh resort?

14. What is a scallion?

15. Which American state wanted R. Dean Taylor in the title of a 1971 hit?

16. What was first tested by Brian Trubshaw?

Answers to page 178
QUIZ 177: **1.** Africa **2.** The Vapors **3.** 400 metres **4.** Green **5.** Helicopter **6.** Dostoevsky **7.** Adams
8. Pottery **9.** *Heartbeat* **10.** Three French hens **11.** The Walker Brothers **12.** Ear, nose and throat
13. Mr Kipling **14.** Farce **15.** A mirage **16.** Jerry Lewis

Quiz 180

Answers on page 179

1. Which prison is located at Princetown?

2. In which city is the Millennium Stadium?

3. In which city do Juventus Football Club play?

4. Which comedy actor's middle name is Marwood?

5. Who directed the 2002 film *Catch Me If You Can*?

6. Michael Flatley was associated with which Irish dance show?

7. Who wrote *2001: A Space Odyssey*?

8. In which country is the Great Slave Lake?

9. Which planet is farthest from the Sun?

10. What percentage of air is oxygen?

11. In which country is the Uluru national park?

12. Which man of many guises had a 1999 number one with 'Praise You'?

13. What did Hoss Cartwright have in common with the Stewart from 10cc?

14. What is a baby kangaroo called?

15. In which city was Michael Owen born?

16. In which country is the ski resort of Sapporo?

Answers to page 179
QUIZ 178: **1.** Battle of the Somme **2.** Mel Gibson **3.** Eight **4.** Black Sea **5.** George Lazenby **6.** Gaia **7.** H.E. Bates **8.** Wycombe Wanderers **9.** Rowland Hill **10.** 1916 **11.** R.E.M. **12.** *Hamlet* **13.** Frans Hals **14.** Jim Laker **15.** Glasgow **16.** Ralph Filthy

Quiz 181

Answers on page 184

1. In which city is the University of East Anglia?

2. Which culinary term, popular in the late 1980s, means 'new cooking'?

3. Which wild flower is also known as heartsease?

4. Pérez de Cuéllar was secretary general of which body from 1982 to 1991?

5. Which band wanted to 'Keep the Faith' in 1992?

6. What was Paddington Bear's favourite food?

7. Which planet has a moon named Charon?

8. How many playing cards are there in a standard pack?

9. Which American state is known as the 'Flickertail State'?

10. In which English county is Kettering?

11. How many celebrity panellists are there on each edition of *Blankety Blank*?

12. North Brabant is a province of which country?

13. Who sang about a 'Cornflake Girl'?

14. What is the singular of 'graffiti'?

15. What is unusual about Jane Austen's novel *Lady Susan*?

16. What is the name for a military morning wake-up call?

Answers to page 184
QUIZ 183: **1.** Northamptonshire **2.** Steve McManaman **3.** 15 **4.** 49 **5.** French Guiana **6.** London
7. Dance **8.** Doges **9.** Betty Grable **10.** Palace of Holyroodhouse **11.** German **12.** Home Counties **13.**
Khmer Rouge **14.** Ireland **15.** Shirley MacLaine **16.** 'My lady'

Quiz 182

Answers on page 185

1. What is Jude's surname in Thomas Hardy's novel *Jude the Obscure*?

2. Which Football League club plays at Sixfields Stadium?

3. In which TV drama series did Nigel Havers succeed Nigel Le Vaillant?

4. Which bird took Manfred Mann to number one in 1966?

5. Which country lies immediately to the south of Angola?

6. Since 1066, which two English kings have been the only monarchs of that name?

7. Which chat show host is *All Talk*?

8. What statue stands in London's Piccadilly Circus?

9. What name is given to an area of open space surrounding a city?

10. In Greek mythology, what sprang up on the spot where Narcissus died?

11. In which American city does hip-hop music have its origins?

12. Opium is extracted from the unripe seeds of which plant?

13. In which century was Charlotte Brontë born?

14. Of which footballer did Sir Alex Ferguson say: 'He could start a row in an empty house'?

15. What were the followers of 14th-century religious reformer John Wycliffe known as?

16. In which other country does London stand on the River Thames?

Answers to page 185
QUIZ 184: **1.** Mauretania **2.** 95% **3.** Melton Mowbray **4.** Loudness **5.** Michael Collins **6.** November **7.** Bird **8.** Remus **9.** Pete Sampras **10.** Maggie Smith **11.** Norfolk **12.** Gerald Durrell **13.** Janus **14.** Scottish country dances **15.** Lillian Gish **16.** Freetown

Quiz 183

Answers on page 182

1. In which county was the Battle of Naseby fought in 1645?

2. Which footballing Steve moved from Liverpool to Real Madrid?

3. How many kings of Sweden were called Charles?

4. How many goals did Bobby Charlton score for England?

5. Off which country does Devil's Island lie?

6. In which English city is St Katherine's Dock?

7. In which field of the arts did Anton Dolin make his name?

8. What were the chief magistrates called in ancient Venice and Genoa?

9. Who starred in the musicals *Follow the Fleet* and *Pin Up Girl*?

10. What is the name of the royal residence in Edinburgh?

11. What nationality was the artist Hans Holbein?

12. What name is given to the counties closest to London?

13. Pol Pot was the leader of which guerrilla movement?

14. In which country is the River Liffey?

15. Which actress is the sister of Warren Beatty?

16. What does Madonna mean?

Answers to page 182
QUIZ 181: **1.** Norwich **2.** Nouvelle cuisine **3.** Wild pansy **4.** United Nations **5.** Bon Jovi
6. Marmalade sandwiches **7.** Pluto **8.** 52 **9.** North Dakota **10.** Northamptonshire **11.** Six
12. Netherlands **13.** Tori Amos **14.** Graffito **15.** It is written in the form of letters **16.** Reveille

Quiz 184

Answers on page 183

1. The ouguiya is the currency of which country?

2. What percentage of a melon is water?

3. Which Leicestershire town is renowned for its pork pies?

4. A phon is a unit of what?

5. Which Irish nationalist leader was assassinated on 22 August 1922?

6. In which month is Remembrance Day?

7. What is a ring ouzel?

8. In Roman legend, who was Romulus's twin brother?

9. In 1990, which tennis player became the youngest winner of the US Open?

10. Who won an Academy Award for her role in *The Prime of Miss Jean Brodie*?

11. In which English county is Thetford?

12. Which naturalist founded Jersey Zoo?

13. Who was the Roman god of doorways and passageways?

14. What are The De'il Among the Tailors, Maxwell's Rant and Petronella?

15. As whom was the actress Lillian de Guiche better known?

16. What is the capital of Sierra Leone?

Answers to page 183
QUIZ 182: **1.** Fawley **2.** Northampton Town **3.** *Dangerfield* **4.** 'Pretty Flamingo' **5.** Namibia
6. Stephen and John **7.** Clive Anderson **8.** Eros **9.** Green belt **10.** A flower **11.** New York **12.** Opium
poppy **13.** 19th **14.** Dennis Wise **15.** Lollards **16.** Canada

Quiz 185

Answers on page 188

1. How many tusks does an adult wart hog have?

2. Which American state is known as the 'Pine Tree State'?

3. How many jumps does each competitor have in an Olympic long jump final?

4. Which two Northern Ireland politicians won the 1998 Nobel Peace Prize?

5. Which Sydney landmark was opened in 1973?

6. Which pungent creature has the Latin name *Mephitis mephitis*?

7. Which footballer was transferred to Newcastle United for a then world record fee of £15 million in 1996?

8. What can be standard, miniature or toy?

9. Which band released the best-selling album *Rumours*?

10. As whom was jazz pianist Ferdinand Joseph La Menthe Morton better known?

11. What nationality was cyclist Eddie Merckx?

12. In which English county is Mablethorpe?

13. Which Filipino politician was known as the 'Iron Butterfly'?

14. Which novelist wrote *Small World* and *Nice Work*?

15. Who succeeded Michael Foot as leader of the Labour Party?

16. In which country is the port of Jedda?

Answers to page 188
QUIZ 187: **1.** James Callaghan **2.** Ron Howard **3.** *The Eagle Has Landed* **4.** R.E.M. **5.** Crilly
6. St Pancras **7.** Sue Devoy **8.** Warren Beatty **9.** Gianfranco Zola **10.** New South Wales **11.** Platypus
12. Red and white **13.** *Turandot* **14.** John Milton **15.** Spain **16.** A marsupial

Quiz 186

Answers on page 189

1. What does Interpol stand for?

2. Which League was formed by the trading cities of northern Europe in the 12th century?

3. Which movie sex symbol of the 1930s changed her name from Harlean Carpentier?

4. Which mythological creatures had women's faces and vultures' bodies?

5. From which country do freesia plants originate?

6. Which actress split from Woody Allen in 1992?

7. What was launched in 11 EU states in 1999?

8. In which field event did American athlete Randy Barnes specialise?

9. Which weasel has dark brown fur and two yellow face patches?

10. Susan Stranks, Mick Robertson and Tommy Boyd all presented which children's TV show?

11. Which band is fronted by the grandson of Sir John Mills?

12. What instrument did Mrs Mills play?

13. Which boxer took the World Heavyweight title from Lennox Lewis in 1994?

14. How many feet are there in a fathom?

15. Which French royal house gave its name to a biscuit?

16. Which athletic competition combines cross-country skiing with rifle shooting?

Answers to page 189
QUIZ 188: **1.** Nigella Lawson **2.** Kinshasa (Zaire) **3.** Antarctica **4.** Willie Ryan **5.** Rudolph Valentino **6.** U Thant **7.** Sundial **8.** Tina Charles **9.** Furniture **10.** 1900 **11.** Denzel Washington **12.** Kent **13.** American **14.** Germany **15.** Julie Christie **16.** An aluminium can with a ring-pull

Quiz 187

Answers on page 186

1. Which British home secretary of 1967–70 went on to become Prime Minister?

2. Which star of *Happy Days* has become a successful movie director?

3. Which 1976 movie starring Michael Caine, Donald Sutherland and Robert Duvall was based on a Jack Higgins best-seller?

4. Michael Stipe is the singer with which band?

5. What was Father Ted's surname?

6. Near which London railway station is the British Library?

7. Which New Zealander recorded a hat-trick of world squash titles from 1990 to 1992?

8. Which actor directed the 1981 Oscar-winning movie *Reds*?

9. Which footballer joined Chelsea from Parma in 1996?

10. In which Australian state is Wagga Wagga?

11. Which mammal was thought to be a fake when first discovered?

12. What two colours feature on the flag of Peru?

13. From which Puccini opera does 'Nessun Dorma' come?

14. Who wrote *Paradise Lost*?

15. The cream of which country's footballers play in the Primera Liga?

16. What is a yapok?

Answers to page 186
QUIZ 185: **1.** Four **2.** Maine **3.** Six **4.** John Hume and David Trimble **5.** Opera House **6.** Skunk **7.** Alan Shearer **8.** Poodle **9.** Fleetwood Mac **10.** Jelly Roll Morton **11.** Belgian **12.** Lincolnshire **13.** Imelda Marcos **14.** David Lodge **15.** Neil Kinnock **16.** Saudi Arabia

Quiz 188

Answers on page 187

1. Which TV cook is the daughter of a former Chancellor of the Exchequer?

2. Which capital city was seized by Tutsi rebels in 1997?

3. Where is the Ross Sea?

4. Who rode Benny the Dip to victory in the 1997 Epsom Derby?

5. Which screen idol's first starring role was in *The Four Horsemen of the Apocalypse*?

6. Which U was secretary general of the United Nations?

7. On what does a gnomon cast a shadow?

8. Which Tina had a seventies hit with 'I Love to Love'?

9. What did Thomas Sheraton design?

10. In which year was the Queen Mother born?

11. Who played boxer Rubin 'Hurricane' Carter in the 1999 movie *The Hurricane*?

12. In which county is Brands Hatch motor-racing circuit?

13. What nationality was the poet Henry Wadsworth Longfellow?

14. Which country forms the western border of the Czech Republic?

15. Who starred in *Billy Liar*, *Darling* and *Dr Zhivago*?

16. What were Iron City Beer of Pittsburgh, Pennsylvania, the first to produce in 1962?

Answers to page 187
QUIZ 186: **1.** International Criminal Police Organisation **2.** Hanseatic League **3.** Jean Harlow **4.** Harpies **5.** South Africa **6.** Mia Farrow **7.** The Euro **8.** Shot put **9.** Wolverine **10.** *Magpie* **11.** Kula Shaker **12.** Piano **13.** Oliver McCall **14.** Six **15.** Bourbon **16.** Biathlon

Quiz 189

Answers on page 192

1. A quarter of the bones in the human body are located in which area?

2. Who is Steve Coogan's Portuguese crooner?

3. Who wrote *Educating Rita* and *Shirley Valentine*?

4. What is a cotoneaster?

5. Blondel was a minstrel friend of which English king?

6. Which English city did the Romans call Venta Bulgarum?

7. How many dogs take part in a greyhound race?

8. A man with what appendage was hired in 1911 to assure passengers that the new escalators on the London Underground were safe to use?

9. Which English monarch reputedly shook hands with the branches of an oak tree in the belief that it was the King of Prussia?

10. What is pogonophobia?

11. Which US state is nicknamed the 'Bear State'?

12. Who were the first father and daughter to sing together on a UK number one?

13. Which war was the backdrop for Stanley Kubrick's 1987 movie *Full Metal Jacket*?

14. In music, how many quavers equal a crotchet?

15. In which sport do some participants wear sheepskin nosebands?

16. Which *Fawlty Towers* dragon is also the scourge of Tesco?

Answers to page 192
QUIZ 191: **1.** *The Catcher in the Rye* **2.** Blue **3.** Sindy **4.** Postman **5.** Feet **6.** Romanian **7.** Mollusc
8. Egypt **9.** Bob Wilson **10.** Renault **11.** Sherlock Holmes **12.** Rastafarianism **13.** Richard II
14. Andy Williams **15.** Roy Rogers **16.** Sea lion

Quiz 190

Answers on page 193

1. Which member of Emerson, Lake and Palmer went solo for a 1975 Christmas hit?

2. What was the pseudonym of playwright Jean-Baptiste Poquelin?

3. In *Brookside*, who married Emily Shadwick in 2001?

4. Which Bulgarian was named European Footballer of the Year in 1994?

5. In which country is Belo Horizonte?

6. Which country's flag features a white crescent and star on a red background?

7. Which is the first classic horse race of the British flat season?

8. Which animal produces 200 times more wind per day than the average human?

9. Which city's branch of Alcoholics Anonymous boasted just two members when it started up in 1948?

10. What followed Mary to school one day?

11. As whom was Julius Marx better known?

12. What mark indicates that a product has been approved by the British Standards Institute?

13. What nationality was suspected spy Mata Hari?

14. Ulan Bator is the capital of which country?

15. Which US President issued a detailed foreign policy doctrine in 1823?

16. Who had a hit with the theme song from *Friends*?

Answers to page 193
QUIZ 192: **1.** The Cavemobile **2.** Perseus **3.** Moroccan **4.** Lupe Velez **5.** Breathalyser **6.** Van Clomp **7.** Austin **8.** Italy **9.** East Grinstead **10.** The Mendips **11.** Wimbledon **12.** Goat **13.** Libel is written defamation, slander is spoken **14.** 1965 **15.** New York **16.** Florence

Quiz 191

Answers on page 190

1. What book was Mark Chapman carrying when he shot John Lennon?

2. What colour Smartie replaced the light brown in 1989?

3. Which female icon didn't own a bath until 1972?

4. What was the job of *Cheers* regular Cliff Clavin?

5. Through which part of their bodies do butterflies taste?

6. What nationality was tennis player Ilie Nastase?

7. What type of creature is a clam?

8. Nefertiti was queen of which country in the 14th century BC?

9. Which male TV presenter's middle name is Primrose?

10. In which make of car did Alain Prost achieve his first Grand Prix win?

11. Basil Rathbone, Peter Cushing and Jeremy Brett have all played which character?

12. Which religion was originally based on the ideas of Marcus Garvey?

13. Which English king was the son of Edward, the Black Prince?

14. Which American singer had his first UK hit for 23 years in 1999?

15. Which TV cowboy had his horse Trigger stuffed and mounted after it died?

16. What animal is Andre in the 1994 film of that name?

Answers to page 190
QUIZ 189: **1.** Feet **2.** Tony Ferrino **3.** Willy Russell **4.** A shrub **5.** Richard I **6.** Winchester **7.** Six **8.** A wooden leg **9.** George III **10.** Fear of beards **11.** Arkansas **12.** Frank and Nancy Sinatra **13.** Vietnam War **14.** Two **15.** Horse racing **16.** Prunella Scales

Quiz 192

Answers on page 191

1. What was the name of the Flintstones' car?

2. In Greek mythology, who rescued and married Andromeda?

3. What nationality is the distance runner Said Aouita?

4. Which Hollywood actress was known as 'The Mexican Spitfire'?

5. Which innovation was originally called the 'drunkometer'?

6. In *'Allo 'Allo*, who painted *The Fallen Madonna with the Big Boobies*?

7. What is the state capital of Texas?

8. Which country has a toe and a heel?

9. Heading due south along the meridian from Greenwich, what is the first town of any note outside Greater London?

10. Cheddar Gorge cuts a swathe through which hills?

11. Which Football League club used to play at Plough Lane?

12. If something is 'caprine', it is like which animal?

13. What is the difference between libel and slander?

14. In which year did Tom Jones reach number one with 'It's Not Unusual'?

15. In which city is the Holland road tunnel?

16. Fiorentina are a football team from which city?

Answers to page 191
QUIZ 190: **1.** Greg Lake **2.** Molière **3.** Timothy O'Leary **4.** Hristo Stoichkov **5.** Brazil **6.** Turkey **7.** One Thousand Guineas **8.** Cow **9.** Luxembourg **10.** Her little lamb **11.** Groucho Marx **12.** Kite mark **13.** Dutch **14.** Mongolia **15.** James Monroe **16.** The Rembrandts

Quiz 193

Answers on page 196

1. Who asked: 'Does Your Chewing Gum Lose Its Flavour (On The Bedpost Overnight)'?

2. How many Epsom Derby winners did Lester Piggott ride?

3. Which 11th-century wizard became stranded in the 20th century?

4. Iago featured in which Shakespeare play?

5. Which trainer's daughter presents the BBC's horse racing coverage?

6. How many court cards are there in a pack of cards?

7. Which legislation banned alcohol in the United States during the 1920s?

8. Which sound indicated a Rank Organisation film?

9. What did the sisters Stheno, Euryale and Medusa have for hair?

10. Who painted *The Supper at Emmaus*?

11. Which phrase means 'through my fault' in Latin?

12. Which TV medical series is a spin-off from *Casualty*?

13. Which band had a 1978 hit with 'Airport'?

14. How many points are there on a backgammon board?

15. Which county's coastline includes Pegwell Bay?

16. Who wrote the novel *The Corrections*?

Answers to page 196
QUIZ 195: **1.** Rome **2.** Agate **3.** Operation Overlord **4.** Frown **5.** Pink **6.** A type of antelope **7.** *Lady Chatterley's Lover* **8.** Washington **9.** *News at Ten* **10.** Valéry **11.** Giles **12.** Annie Lennox **13.** Lauren Bacall **14.** 'Little Green Apples' **15.** 12th **16.** Robert Burns

Quiz 194

Answers on page 197

1. Which is the deepest canyon in North America?

2. Which religious order was founded by Ignatius Loyola?

3. Septime is a position in which sport?

4. What is the capital of Trinidad and Tobago?

5. Which is the second largest English county?

6. Which island is also known as Lindisfarne?

7. Whose second novel was entitled *The Autograph Man*?

8. Juneau is the capital of which American state?

9. What links William Shakespeare, Ingrid Bergman and former England football manager Joe Mercer?

10. Who was the local butcher in *Dad's Army*?

11. Which horse won the Grand National for the third time in 1977?

12. Who played Himmler in the film *The Eagle Has Landed*?

13. Which title did Austria's Eva Rueber-Staier win in 1969?

14. Which brand of disinfectant took its name from London sanitary engineer Harry Pickup?

15. Which English king reigned from 1272 to 1307?

16. Which much-married American actor's real name is Joe Yule Jnr?

Answers to page 197
QUIZ 196: **1.** Venus **2.** All are former policemen **3.** Transport and General Workers' Union **4.** *As Good as It Gets* **5.** Melinda Messenger **6.** Yachting **7.** Ambrosia **8.** Peter Benchley **9.** HMS *Victory* **10.** The Attractions **11.** Spain **12.** Sweep with it – it's a kind of broom **13.** Tomatoes **14.** Edward VIII **15.** Desert rat **16.** Timmy

Quiz 195

Answers on page 194

1. Which city was sacked in 410?

2. What is the birthstone for the month of June?

3. What was the codename for the D-Day landings?

4. Which requires the use of more facial muscles – a smile or a frown?

5. What colour is yak's milk?

6. What is a gemsbok?

7. Which D.H. Lawrence novel was banned until November 1960?

8. In which American state is Mount St Helens?

9. Which TV news programme began in 1967?

10. What was the Christian name of the French President Giscard d'Estaing?

11. Which newspaper cartoonist created a family built around the formidable Grandma?

12. Which singer's 1992 album was titled *Diva*?

13. Which Hollywood actress was Miss Greenwich Village of 1942?

14. Which fruit did Roger Miller sing about in 1968?

15. In which century did beavers become extinct in the UK?

16. Which Scottish poet wrote two poems about his pet ewe called Poor Mailie?

Answers to page 194
QUIZ 193: **1.** Lonnie Donegan **2.** Nine **3.** Catweazle **4.** *Othello* **5.** Clare Balding **6.** 12 **7.** Prohibition **8.** Gong **9.** Snakes **10.** Caravaggio **11.** Mea culpa **12.** *Holby City* **13.** The Motors **14.** 24 **15.** Kent **16.** Jonathan Franzen

Quiz 196

Answers on page 195

1. Which planet has the longest day?

2. What job links Christopher Dean, Geoff Capes and Dave Dee?

3. What does TGWU stand for?

4. Jack Nicholson and Helen Hunt both won Oscars in 1997 for their performances in which film?

5. Which model presents *Fort Boyard*?

6. In which sport do countries compete for the America's Cup?

7. Which food of the Greek gods was supposed to confer eternal life upon all who ate it?

8. Who wrote the novel of *Jaws*?

9. Which flagship of Nelson's sits in dock at Portsmouth?

10. Which group often backed Elvis Costello?

11. Vigo is a port in which country?

12. What would you do with a besom?

13. Which fruits used to be known as 'love apples'?

14. Which English king abdicated in 1936?

15. Which creature has sex up to 122 times per hour?

16. What was the name of the dog in Enid Blyton's *Famous Five* books?

Answers to page 195
QUIZ 194: **1.** Hell's Canyon **2.** The Jesuits **3.** Fencing **4.** Port of Spain **5.** Cumbria **6.** Holy Island **7.** Zadie Smith **8.** Alaska **9.** All died on their birthdays **10.** Corporal Jones **11.** Red Rum **12.** Donald Pleasence **13.** Miss World **14.** Harpic **15.** Edward I **16.** Mickey Rooney

Quiz 197

Answers on page 200

1. Which TV detective kept a pet alligator named Elvis?

2. What can be a colour or a loud cry in pursuit of a criminal?

3. In which county is Aylesbury?

4. Who was the only English monarch to be a member of the House of Saxe-Coburg?

5. What was the Christian name of the British sculptor Moore?

6. Which was the first product to be advertised on the opening night of ITV in September 1955?

7. Which grand old soldier had 10,000 men?

8. On which island is Mount Etna?

9. What is the capital of the Falkland Islands?

10. Which Australian golfer is nicknamed the 'Great White Shark'?

11. Which Dutch artist once taught languages and maths at a school in Ramsgate?

12. Cornish Yarg cheese is traditionally served coated in what?

13. In which national park did Yogi Bear live?

14. Which football club won the Danish League title in 2001?

15. Of what musical instrument are you afraid if you suffer from aulophobia?

16. Who played the second Doctor Who?

Answers to page 200
QUIZ 199: **1.** Walk on dry land **2.** 1942 **3.** Noah **4.** Tony Christie **5.** Neil **6.** Wrexham (v Arsenal) **7.** Herman and Lily Munster **8.** Joe Louis **9.** Manuel Noriega **10.** Around the north of Canada **11.** George V **12.** Luton **13.** Six **14.** Stephen Sondheim **15.** Jimmy Somerville **16.** Surrey

Quiz 198

Answers on page 201

1. Which former Radio 1 disc jockey was named Pipe Smoker of the Year in 1982?

2. What did George Burns, Irving Berlin and Hal Roach have in common?

3. Which English comedian was awarded the freedom of the capital city of Albania?

4. Who shot Phil Mitchell in *EastEnders* in 2001?

5. If something is cerebral, to what part of the body does it pertain?

6. Who was the singer with Frankie Goes to Hollywood?

7. What is unusual about the populations of Australia, Mongolia and New Zealand?

8. Which footballer was known as 'The Black Panther'?

9. What was the biggest-selling toy of 1957?

10. In which country was the artist Chagall born?

11. Who traditionally lives at 11 Downing Street?

12. Which actress won a 1972 Academy Award for Best Actress for *Cabaret*?

13. Who was Gary's first flatmate in *Men Behaving Badly*?

14. Where is the volcano Olympus Mons?

15. Which Prime Minister's father-in-law used to be a 'randy Scouse git'?

16. Which is the world's second smallest state?

Answers to page 201
QUIZ 200: **1.** *Midnight Cowboy* **2.** Dingwall **3.** Rabbit **4.** David Vine **5.** Dustin Hoffman and Jon Voight **6.** 'Achy Breaky Heart' **7.** Juan Carlos **8.** Swiss **9.** Hitler **10.** The emperor **11.** Penelope **12.** Blair General **13.** Samantha Morton **14.** Steve Redgrave **15.** St John's **16.** Newt

Quiz 199

Answers on page 198

1. What can a mudskipper do that other fish can't?

2. In which year was the Battle of El Alamein?

3. In the Old Testament, who was the father of Shem, Ham and Japheth?

4. Which singer maintained that he did what he did for Maria?

5. Which member of The Young Ones had a hit with 'Hole in my Shoe'?

6. In January 1992, who became the first team finishing bottom of the Football League the previous season to knock the reigning champions out of the FA Cup?

7. Who were the first American sitcom couple to be seen regularly sharing a bed on TV?

8. Which boxer was known as 'The Brown Bomber'?

9. Which Panama ruler was arrested in 1989 following an American invasion of the country?

10. Where is the Northwest Passage?

11. Who was the first British monarch from the House of Windsor?

12. Which Bedfordshire town used to be synonymous with hat-making?

13. How many points is the pink ball in snooker worth?

14. Who wrote the lyrics of *West Side Story*?

15. Who was the lead singer with Bronski Beat on 'Smalltown Boy'?

16. Which county cricket club have their headquarters at The Oval?

Answers to page 198
QUIZ 197: **1.** 'Sonny' Crockett (*Miami Vice*) **2.** Hue **3.** Buckinghamshire **4.** Edward VII **5.** Henry **6.** Gibbs' SR toothpaste **7.** Duke of York **8.** Sicily **9.** Stanley **10.** Greg Norman **11.** Van Gogh **12.** Nettles **13.** Yellowstone **14.** FC Copenhagen **15.** Flute **16.** Patrick Troughton

Quiz 200

Answers on page 199

1. John Schlesinger won a 1969 Academy Award for directing which movie?

2. In which town do Scottish football team Ross County play their home matches?

3. Coney is the fur of which animal?

4. Who was the first host of *A Question of Sport*?

5. Who were the two main male actors in *Midnight Cowboy*?

6. What was Billy Ray Cyrus suffering from in 1992?

7. Who became King of Spain in 1975?

8. What nationality was the psychiatrist Carl Jung?

9. The July Conspiracy was an unsuccessful plot to assassinate which dictator?

10. Which is the largest breed of penguin?

11. According to Greek legend, who was the wife of Odysseus?

12. At which hospital did *Dr Kildare* work?

13. Which actress starred alongside Tom Cruise in 2002's *Minority Report*?

14. Who was BBC Sports Personality of the Year for 2000?

15. What is the capital of Newfoundland?

16. Crested, smooth and palmate are all types of what?

Answers to page 199
QUIZ 198: **1.** Dave Lee Travis **2.** They all lived to be 100 **3.** Norman Wisdom **4.** Lisa Shaw **5.** Brain **6.** Holly Johnson **7.** There are more sheep than humans **8.** Eusebio **9.** The hula hoop **10.** Russia **11.** Chancellor of the Exchequer **12.** Liza Minnelli **13.** Dermot **14.** Mars **15.** Tony Blair (father-in-law Tony Booth played Liverpudlian Mike in *Till Death Us Do Part*) **16.** Monaco

Quiz 201

Answers on page 204

1. Which actor quit making films with Francis the Talking Mule after learning that the mule received more fan mail than him?

2. Which birds are trained to catch and retrieve fish in China?

3. What can't an owl parrot do that other owls and parrots can?

4. Which grow faster – fingernails or toenails?

5. Which planet has daytime temperatures as high as 800 degrees Fahrenheit but has ice at its poles?

6. Which rap artist was born Robert Van Winkle?

7. In which country was Mel Gibson born?

8. What sport is played by the Sheffield Steelers and the Nottingham Panthers?

9. Which country boasts a Gold Coast?

10. In which city do the Royle Family live?

11. According to Ibiza superstition, it is bad luck to allow what on a fishing boat?

12. Who was Britain's first black woman newsreader?

13. What is siderophobia?

14. Which boxer was nicknamed 'Gentleman Jim'?

15. What was 8 May 1945 otherwise known as?

16. In which sport do European club sides play for the Heineken Cup?

Answers to page 204
QUIZ 203: **1.** Ali G **2.** Ionian **3.** The Ivy League **4.** Copernicus **5.** Catherine Cookson **6.** 8,000 **7.** Prefab Sprout **8.** LXV **9.** Talbot Rothwell **10.** Charlie Hungerford **11.** Tiger Woods **12.** Show-jumping **13.** Mecca **14.** Plaid Cymru **15.** Enya **16.** Pisces

Quiz 202

Answers on page 205

1. Which Scottish island was evacuated on 29 August 1930?

2. Where did both Maria Muldaur and the Brand New Heavies spend Midnight?

3. What is the birthstone for November?

4. What sport do the Chicago Bulls play?

5. Who discovered the Victoria Falls?

6. Which comedians revived *Randall & Hopkirk (Deceased)*?

7. Who cut off Samson's hair?

8. Which American city is headquarters of the Mormon Church?

9. On which golf course is the World Matchplay Championship held?

10. From which Dumfries and Galloway port would you catch a ferry to Larne in Northern Ireland?

11. In 1985, which two clubs became the first to share a ground in the history of the Football League?

12. People with what colour hair have more hairs on their head than any other?

13. In which European country was cheese a form of currency in the 16th century?

14. How many brains does a leech have?

15. Who starred with Michelle Pfeiffer in *Frankie and Johnny*?

16. Who wrote *The Shining* and *Pet Sematary*?

Answers to page 205
QUIZ 204: **1.** Western Australia **2.** Italian **3.** Almond **4.** Pitcher **5.** One eye **6.** A coal fire
7. Coatbridge **8.** Baron Greenback **9.** The Old Vic **10.** Missouri **11.** Eddie Irvine **12.** Ordnance Survey
13. House of Orange **14.** Richard II **15.** Charles Laughton **16.** Bridge Street

Quiz 203

Answers on page 202

1. Who is Sacha Baron Cohen's first famous creation?

2. In which sea is the island of Ithaca?

3. What league was originally made up of the American universities of Harvard, Yale, Columbia and Brown?

4. Who declared in 1543 that the Sun was at the centre of the Universe?

5. Which novelist wrote *Tilly Trotter* and *The Glass Virgin*?

6. What is the cube of 20?

7. Paddy McAloon is the singer with which band?

8. What is the Roman number for 65?

9. Who wrote *Up Pompeii!* and most of the *Carry On* films?

10. Who was Jim Bergerac's father-in-law?

11. Which golfer won the 1997 US Masters by a record 12 shots?

12. Hickstead is synonymous with which sport?

13. Which city was the birthplace of Muhammad?

14. What is the name of the Welsh nationalist party?

15. Which Irish singer had a 1988 number one with 'Orinoco Flow'?

16. Which star sign follows Aquarius?

Answers to page 202
QUIZ 201: **1.** Donald O'Connor **2.** Cormorants **3.** Fly **4.** Fingernails **5.** Mercury **6.** Vanilla Ice **7.** USA **8.** Ice hockey **9.** Australia **10.** Manchester **11.** A priest **12.** Moira Stuart **13.** A fear of the stars **14.** James J. Corbett **15.** V-E Day **16.** Rugby Union

Quiz 204

Answers on page 203

1. In which Australian state is the town of Albany?

2. What nationality were the group Black Box who had a UK number one with 'Ride On Time'?

3. What nuts are used to make marzipan?

4. What can be a large vessel, a carnivorous plant or a baseball thrower?

5. What part of Rex Harrison's anatomy was made of glass?

6. If there were French nuts in your lounge, what would you have?

7. In which Scottish town do the football team Albion Rovers play?

8. Which toad was the arch enemy of Dangermouse?

9. Which London theatre was home to the National Theatre from 1963 to 1976?

10. On which river does Omaha stand?

11. Which British driver drove for Jaguar in Formula One in 2001?

12. Which body was previously known as the Trigonometrical Survey?

13. Which Dutch royal family took their name from a small principality in southern France?

14. Which English king was faced with the Peasants' Revolt?

15. Who starred in *Mutiny on the Bounty* and *The Hunchback of Notre Dame*?

16. In which street is the café in *EastEnders*?

Answers to page 203
QUIZ 202: **1.** St Kilda **2.** At The Oasis **3.** Topaz **4.** Basketball **5.** David Livingstone **6.** Reeves and Mortimer **7.** Delilah **8.** Salt Lake City **9.** Wentworth **10.** Stranraer **11.** Crystal Palace and Charlton **12.** Blonde **13.** Denmark **14.** 32 **15.** Al Pacino **16.** Stephen King

Quiz 205

Answers on page 208

1. Which animal has no vocal cords?

2. Which actor who starred in *Edward Scissorhands* has a phobia about clowns?

3. Which are the only birds that can see the colour blue?

4. Which band had a 1982 hit with 'Abracadabra'?

5. Which world motor-racing champion was killed in a car crash on the Guildford by-pass in 1959?

6. Who is leader of the Staines Massive?

7. Which one-time resident of Gravesend was the subject of a 1995 Disney film?

8. On which gulf is the town of Sorrento?

9. Who had his own Velvet Opera?

10. What is the American term for grilling food?

11. Scrooge featured in which Dickens novel?

12. Which tea party was the topic of a 1976 song by The Sensational Alex Harvey Band?

13. Who was 'The It Girl'?

14. Who created the detective Jemima Shore?

15. Which country's currency is the tenge?

16. What was the name of *Hector Heathcote*'s faithful dog?

Answers to page 208
QUIZ 207: **1.** On the wing **2.** The Sorbonne **3.** *Roget's Thesaurus* **4.** 38th parallel **5.** Ermintrude
6. 1989–90 **7.** Right Said Fred **8.** Jethro Tull **9.** Calvin Coolidge **10.** Conductor **11.** *Home and Away*
12. Golf **13.** Karate **14.** Rex Hunt **15.** A venomous snake **16.** Michael Jackson

Quiz 206

Answers on page 209

1. What stretches from West Gansu to the Gulf of Liaodong?

2. Which bridge in eastern England was the longest single-span suspension bridge in the world when it was completed in 1980?

3. The poisonous plant deadly nightshade belongs to the same family as which vegetable?

4. What is the name for a pregnant goldfish?

5. In which group of islands is Martinique?

6. What canal, spelt backwards, is the name of a Greek god?

7. What is the name of Ricky Gervais's character in *The Office*?

8. What are the Christian names of tennis's Williams sisters?

9. Which English city has a Hoe and a Sound?

10. Which politician was labelled 'Attila the Hen'?

11. Who played Yosser Hughes in *Boys From the Blackstuff*?

12. What is 'Buzz' Aldrin's real first name?

13. What nationality was the author Hilaire Belloc?

14. What is campanology?

15. A sousaphone is a large bass version of which musical instrument?

16. Who was quite contrary?

Quiz 207

Answers on page 206

1. Where do swifts mate?

2. What is the University of Paris commonly known as?

3. Which collection of synonyms was first published in 1852?

4. Along which line of latitude is the border between North and South Korea based?

5. What was the name of the cow in *The Magic Roundabout*?

6. In which season did Liverpool Football Club last win the League title?

7. Who were 'Deeply Dippy' in 1992?

8. Which 18th-century agriculturist was not living in the past when he wrote *Horse-Hoeing Husbandry*?

9. Which Calvin became US President in 1923?

10. What was Herbert von Karajan?

11. Which TV soap is set in Summer Bay?

12. Which sport does Lee Westwood play?

13. Which martial art takes its name from the Japanese for 'empty hand'?

14. Who was governor of the Falklands at the time of the Argentine invasion?

15. What was the speckled band in the Sherlock Holmes story of that title?

16. Whose 1987 album was *Bad*?

Answers to page 206
QUIZ 205: **1.** Giraffe **2.** Johnny Depp **3.** Owls **4.** The Steve Miller Band **5.** Mike Hawthorn **6.** Ali G **7.** Pocahontas **8.** Gulf of Salerno **9.** Elmer Gantry **10.** Broiling **11.** *A Christmas Carol* **12.** 'The Boston Tea Party' **13.** Clara Bow **14.** Antonia Fraser **15.** Kazakhstan **16.** Winston

Quiz 208

Answers on page 207

1. What do oysters change depending on the temperature of the water around them?

2. What are the two main ingredients of zabaglione?

3. Who was Anastasia and Drizella's stepsister?

4. What is the highest mountain outside Asia?

5. What is the second largest desert in the world?

6. Who wrote *A Woman of Substance* and *Hold the Dream*?

7. In which sport do teams compete for the Stanley Cup?

8. In *The Bill,* which is the nearest station to Sun Hill?

9. In which century did Ivan the Terrible reign?

10. Which boy's name is sweet when applied to a member of the *Dianthus* family?

11. For which organisation did *The Champions* work?

12. In which year was Damon Hill Formula One World Champion?

13. Who was 'Gonna Make You A Star' in 1974?

14. Who was the first *Blue Peter* pet?

15. Which TV presenter conducts *Weird Weekends*?

16. In which city is the Rialto bridge?

Answers to page 207
QUIZ 206: **1.** Great Wall of China **2.** Humber Bridge **3.** The potato **4.** Twit **5.** West Indies **6.** Suez **7.** David Brent **8.** Venus and Serena **9.** Plymouth **10.** Margaret Thatcher **11.** Bernard Hill **12.** Edwin **13.** English **14.** Bell-ringing **15.** Tuba **16.** Mary

Quiz 209

Answers on page 212

1. For which Jersey police department did Jim Bergerac work?

2. Which acid occurs in stinging ants?

3. Which seventies rock star was born Vince Furnier?

4. What was the name of the milkman in *Camberwick Green*?

5. Which West End musical star once played Caroline Winthrop in *Crossroads*?

6. How many yards are there in a furlong?

7. What are Razor strop and Jew's ear types of?

8. Which music-hall comedian made famous the song 'I Belong to Glasgow'?

9. Which one-hit wonder had a 1980 chart-topper with 'Together We Are Beautiful'?

10. In which year did British war-time rationing end on butter, bacon and meat?

11. What do gibbons, foxes and swans have in common?

12. Which venomous spider gets its name from a town in Italy?

13. What is Rupert Murdoch's first name?

14. Which US President was known as 'The Accidental President'?

15. Which Australian Prime Minister played himself in Barry Humphries' 1974 film *Barry McKenzie Holds His Own*?

16. Which country's rugby union team are called the Springboks?

Answers to page 212
QUIZ 211: **1.** Isotope **2.** *Peak Practice* **3.** Spa-Francorchamps **4.** Windward Islands **5.** The Rebel Rousers **6.** Colombo **7.** Portuguese **8.** They're all green **9.** Michael, Peter and Tom **10.** Centaur **11.** Tutankhamen **12.** Archimedes **13.** Napoleon **14.** A freshwater fish **15.** St Mary's **16.** Kajagoogoo

Quiz 210

Answers on page 213

1. Who wrote *Hay Fever* and *Private Lives*?
2. Who had a 1998 number one with 'Brimful Of Asha'?
3. What is a cowrie?
4. From what were London, Durham and Winchester omitted in 1086?
5. Which author of a book of British battleaxes is married to the former MP for Tatton?
6. What does 'Dodecanese' mean, as in the group of Greek islands?
7. What is the chemical formula for carbon dioxide?
8. In which county is Wookey Hole?
9. What was the name of the poet William Wordsworth's sister?
10. What is the name of the pub in *Emmerdale*?
11. Which Football League team plays at Sincil Bank?
12. Who founded the Amstrad electronics company?
13. Which British acting knight was born Lewis Ernest Watts?
14. Which blockbuster won the Oscar for Best Film in 1997?
15. In which book did Ian Fleming introduce James Bond?
16. What did Hugh Hefner launch in 1953?

Answers to page 213
QUIZ 212: **1.** Germany **2.** Mullard Furniture Industries **3.** Jack Benny **4.** Campion **5.** He was the first substitute to be used in a Football League game **6.** Frisian Islands **7.** A nocturnal bird **8.** They're all carnivorous plants **9.** South Africa **10.** Crowded House **11.** Treaty of Versailles **12.** Whitehorse **13.** A small, triangular bone at the base of the human spine **14.** Denny Hulme **15.** Keats **16.** 17th

Quiz 211

Answers on page 210

1. What term in physics was first coined by Frederick Soddy?

2. Which TV medical drama is set in Cardale?

3. In Formula One, on which circuit is the Belgian Grand Prix staged?

4. Which group of islands are known as the 'Iles du Vent' by the French?

5. Which group backed Cliff Bennett in the 1960s?

6. What is the capital of Sri Lanka?

7. What is the official language of Brazil?

8. What do Kermit, Orville and Dipsy have in common?

9. Which three generations of the Scudamore family have become National Hunt jockeys?

10. Which creature in Greek mythology was half-human and half-horse?

11. Whose tomb was opened in 1922?

12. Who shouted 'Eureka' over what he had discovered in the bath?

13. Who defeated Russian Tsar Alexander I at Austerlitz in 1805?

14. What is a barbel?

15. Which is the largest of the Isles of Scilly?

16. Which band were 'Too Shy' in 1983?

Answers to page 210
QUIZ 209: **1.** Bureau des Etrangers **2.** Formic acid **3.** Alice Cooper **4.** Thomas Tripp **5.** Elaine Paige **6.** 220 **7.** Fungi **8.** Will Fyffe **9.** Fern Kinney **10.** 1954 **11.** They all mate for life **12.** Tarantula (Taranto) **13.** Keith **14.** John Tyler **15.** Gough Whitlam **16.** South Africa

Quiz 212

Answers on page 211

1. In which country was the world's first motorway?

2. What does MFI stand for?

3. Of which US comedian did Fred Allen once say: 'He couldn't ad-lib a belch after a goulash'?

4. Which TV detective had a manservant by the name of Magersfontein Lugg?

5. What landmark was created by Charlton Athletic footballer Keith Peacock on 21 August 1965?

6. Texel is the largest of which group of islands?

7. What is a frogmouth?

8. What do the bladderwort, sundew and pitcher plant have in common?

9. In which country is Sun City?

10. Which band took their name from a cramped apartment they once shared?

11. Which 1919 peace treaty between the Allies and Germany officially ended the First World War?

12. What is the capital of Canada's Yukon territory?

13. What is a coccyx?

14. Which New Zealand driver was Formula One World Champion in 1967?

15. Which poet wrote 'Endymion'?

16. In which century did Sir Isaac Newton formulate his theory of gravitation?

Answers to page 211
QUIZ 210: **1.** Noël Coward **2.** Cornershop **3.** A marine snail **4.** The Domesday Book **5.** Christine Hamilton **6.** 'Twelve islands' **7.** CO_2 **8.** Somerset **9.** Dorothy **10.** The Woolpack **11.** Lincoln City **12.** Alan Sugar **13.** Sir John Mills **14.** *Titanic* **15.** *Casino Royale* **16.** *Playboy*

Quiz 213

Answers on page 216

1. Who hit *The Big Time* after changing her name from Shirley Orr?

2. Which planet was first located in 1930?

3. Jacob's Creek is a brand name of wine from which country?

4. Which university did Prince William enrol at in 2001?

5. What is a satsuma?

6. Who won the Mr Universe contest in 1969?

7. Which church was founded in 1955 by L. Ron Hubbard?

8. Which sport has periods of play called chukkas?

9. The Tokens and Tight Fit both had hits with which tribal song?

10. Which Hollywood star gurgled Maggie Simpson's first words on *The Simpsons*?

11. Of which fellow actor did Helena Bonham Carter say: 'His mouth is a no-go area. It's like kissing the Berlin Wall'?

12. Which is farther east, Crete or Cyprus?

13. The town of Cairns is in which Australian state?

14. Where did Twizzle live?

15. Which group of birds collect in a charm?

16. Whose 2002 album was titled *Escapology*?

Answers to page 216
QUIZ 215: **1.** Isle of Wight **2.** Tonic **3.** Canoeing **4.** Cher and B.A. Robertson **5.** Dudley Moore **6.** Baron **7.** Brownsea Island **8.** Sylvester **9.** Doug Digby **10.** North America **11.** 20 **12.** Mount Kosciusko **13.** Muriel Spark **14.** The Speaker **15.** Chelsea **16.** Quito (Ecuador)

Quiz 214

Answers on page 217

1. *The Lancet* is the journal of which profession?

2. An appearance in which TV soap was the prize awaiting the winners in *Soapstars*?

3. At the 1984 Olympics which athlete took gold in the 100 and 200 metres, the long jump and the sprint relay?

4. In which English city is the Walker Art Gallery?

5. Which disco diva had a 1977 number one with 'I Feel Love'?

6. Who wrote *Watership Down*?

7. The Cambrian mountains are a range in which country?

8. In which sport is a drive prone to a shank or a slice?

9. Which city stages an annual Goose Fair?

10. What do Sandra Bullock, Bill Cosby and Bruce Willis have in common?

11. Which singer's 2001 album was titled *No Angel*?

12. In which continent is Eritrea?

13. Which American state is immediately south of South Dakota?

14. What are the administrative districts in France called?

15. Rockhopper and jackass are species of which bird?

16. What is a saluki?

Answers to page 217
QUIZ 216: **1.** Nicholas Breakspear (Adrian IV) **2.** Mark Morrison **3.** Horse **4.** Ex gratia **5.** *Going Straight* **6.** West **7.** Kornelia Ender **8.** Unit of work **9.** Malcolm Fraser **10.** Gulls **11.** White River **12.** Georgy Porgy **13.** Chris Carter **14.** Jack **15.** Neil Jordan **16.** Jamie Oliver

Quiz 215

Answers on page 214

1. Spithead is a safe anchorage between the coast of England and which island?

2. What can be a pick-me-up or the key note of music scale?

3. In which sport would you use an Eskimo roll?

4. Which two artists had UK top ten hits with songs titled 'Bang Bang'?

5. Which diminutive actor was nicknamed the 'Sex Thimble'?

6. Which is the lowest rank of the British peerage?

7. Which island off Dorset is one of the last British refuges of the red squirrel?

8. Who was Tweety Pie's arch enemy?

9. Who met his death by being impaled on one of his own javelins in *The Grimleys*?

10. The Jerusalem artichoke is a native of which continent?

11. How many times more sensitive are dogs' noses than humans'?

12. Which is the highest mountain in Australia?

13. Who wrote *The Prime of Miss Jean Brodie*?

14. Who keeps order in the House of Commons?

15. Which club won the FA Cup in 1997 and 2000?

16. Which capital city is nearest to the equator?

Answers to page 214
QUIZ 213: **1.** Sheena Easton **2.** Pluto **3.** Australia **4.** St Andrews **5.** A fruit **6.** Arnold Schwarzenegger **7.** Church of Scientology **8.** Polo **9.** 'The Lion Sleeps Tonight' **10.** Elizabeth Taylor **11.** Woody Allen **12.** Cyprus **13.** Queensland **14.** Stray Town **15.** Goldfinches **16.** Robbie Williams

Quiz 216

Answers on page 215

1. Who was the only English Pope?

2. Which singer was sent to prison in 1998 after getting an impostor to do his community service?

3. What sort of animal was the star of *My Friend Flicka*?

4. Which Latin phrase literally means 'from favour'?

5. Which sequel to *Porridge* saw Fletcher released from prison?

6. Bombay is on which coast of India?

7. Which West German swimmer won four gold medals at the 1976 Olympics?

8. What is an erg?

9. Which Australian Prime Minister was nicknamed 'The Prefect'?

10. What can be black-headed, herring or common?

11. On which river does the city of Indianapolis stand?

12. Who kissed the girls and made them cry?

13. Who created *The X Files*?

14. What is the name of the white ball in bowls?

15. Who directed *Interview with the Vampire* and *Michael Collins*?

16. Who opened a restaurant called Fifteen in 2002?

Answers to page 215

QUIZ 214: **1.** Medical **2.** *Emmerdale* **3.** Carl Lewis **4.** Liverpool **5.** Donna Summer **6.** Richard Adams **7.** Wales **8.** Golf **9.** Nottingham **10.** All used to work as bartenders **11.** Dido **12.** Africa **13.** Nebraska **14.** Cantons **15.** Penguin **16.** A breed of dog

Quiz 217

Answers on page 220

1. Which is the only breed of dog that can contract gout?

2. How many letters are there in the Cambodian alphabet?

3. In which English county is the seaside town of Hunstanton?

4. Which Radio 1 DJ married Fatboy Slim?

5. Who received an unprecedented nine sixes at the 1984 Winter Olympics?

6. What species of bird can be Dartford, grasshopper or reed?

7. Which *EastEnders* actress was one of The Hello Girls?

8. Which Spanish artist painted *The Transformation of Narcissus*?

9. What was the Mashed Potato?

10. Which London Underground line serves Heathrow Airport?

11. On which island is Las Palmas?

12. Which two English football clubs are nicknamed the 'Magpies'?

13. Which American state is immediately to the west of New Mexico?

14. Which soap celebrated its 30th birthday in 2002?

15. Which Julie Andrews film won the Best Picture Oscar for 1965?

16. Who wrote *The Camomile Lawn*?

Answers to page 220
QUIZ 219: **1.** Kibbutz **2.** Jeanette Winterson **3.** Goodwood **4.** Thursday **5.** Rula Lenska **6.** Errol Flynn
7. Fear of train travel (siderodromophobia) **8.** Alan Freeman **9.** Tchaikovsky **10.** James
11. Anastasia, daughter of Russian Tsar Nicholas II **12.** Louis XIV **13.** Isle of Dogs **14.** Yemen
15. Ice-T **16.** Generous

Quiz 218

Answers on page 221

1. Which duo comprised Vince Clarke and Alison Moyet?

2. Which Chris Morris TV programme landed in hot water in 2001?

3. According to a recent survey, 7% of Americans think who is still alive?

4. Which is the most westerly city on the African mainland?

5. Which Scottish football club plays in Cumbernauld?

6. Who had a US number one in 1974 with 'I Can Help'?

7. What is the world's best-selling book?

8. In which country is the Hekla volcano?

9. Who won a Best Actress Oscar in 1999 for *Boys Don't Cry*?

10. Who announced at the end of each episode of *The Magic Roundabout* that it was 'Time for bed'?

11. On which Mediterranean island is the port of Famagusta?

12. What does an aurist study?

13. On which sport is Alex Hay a TV commentator?

14. Whose 2001 album was titled *Whoa Nelly*?

15. Fiver and Hazel were characters in which novel?

16. What in Britain are fallow, roe or red?

Answers to page 221
QUIZ 220: **1.** A tortoise **2.** Utopia **3.** Niger **4.** Big Brother **5.** Two by two **6.** Norfolk **7.** Kevin Kennedy (Curly Watts) **8.** Saxophone **9.** Jocky Wilson **10.** Kent **11.** Peak District **12.** They are the same person **13.** Sussex **14.** Sizewell **15.** Meat Loaf **16.** Mark McManus

Quiz 219

Answers on page 218

1. What is the name for a communal settlement in Israel?

2. Who wrote *Oranges Are Not the Only Fruit*?

3. The Stewards' Cup is run on which racecourse?

4. On which day of the week do British elections take place?

5. Which TV actress of Polish descent was born Roza Maria Lubienska?

6. Which Hollywood swashbuckler once worked as a sheep-castrator?

7. What phobia did Sigmund Freud suffer from?

8. Which veteran DJ is known as 'Fluff'?

9. Which composer used to hold his chin with his left hand and conduct with his right because he was afraid his head would roll off his shoulders?

10. What is Paul McCartney's first name?

11. As whom did Anna Anderson pass herself off?

12. Which French monarch reigned for 72 years?

13. Which island is on the opposite side of the Thames from Greenwich Pier?

14. Which country owns the island of Socotra?

15. Which rap artist was born Tracy Marrow?

16. Which horse did Alan Munro ride to victory in the 1991 Derby?

Answers to page 218
QUIZ 217: **1.** Dalmatian **2.** 74 **3.** Norfolk **4.** Zoe Ball **5.** Torvill and Dean **6.** Warbler **7.** Letitia Dean **8.** Salvador Dali **9.** A dance **10.** Piccadilly Line **11.** Gran Canaria **12.** Newcastle United and Notts County **13.** Arizona **14.** *Emmerdale* **15.** *The Sound of Music* **16.** Mary Wesley

Quiz 220

Answers on page 219

1. What pet was re-named 'Wheely' after being fitted with a Lego leg in 1994?

2. Which ideal commonwealth was invented by Sir Thomas More?

3. Which is the third longest river in Africa?

4. Who ruled in *Nineteen Eighty-Four*?

5. In what formation did the animals enter Noah's Ark?

6. In which county in England would you find the Broads?

7. Which *Coronation Street* actor was a helper on *Cheggers Plays Pop*?

8. What instrument did Charlie Parker play?

9. Which Scotsman won the first World Professional Darts Championship?

10. Lydd Airport is in which English county?

11. Kinder Scout is the highest point of which national park?

12. What links the authors Harry Patterson and Jack Higgins?

13. For which county cricket team did Ted Dexter play?

14. What is the name of the nuclear power station in Suffolk?

15. Whose biggest-selling album was *Bat Out of Hell*?

16. Who played Taggart?

Answers to page 219
QUIZ 218: **1.** Yazoo **2.** *Brass Eye* **3.** Elvis Presley **4.** Dakar **5.** Clyde **6.** Billy Swan **7.** The Bible **8.** Iceland **9.** Hilary Swank **10.** Zebedee **11.** Cyprus **12.** Ears **13.** Golf **14.** Nelly Furtado **15.** *Watership Down* **16.** Deer

Quiz 221

Answers on page 224

1. Who wrote *The Glass Menagerie*?

2. Which Hollywood beauty used to work as a weather-girl on *Sun Up*, a San Diego breakfast show?

3. What nationality is Placido Domingo?

4. In which year did Margaret Thatcher become Prime Minister?

5. Which Scottish football team play in Kirkcaldy?

6. Which band were Annie Lennox and Dave Stewart in before The Eurythmics?

7. Where would you encounter Slartibartfast?

8. Which country is also known as the Friendly Islands?

9. The Tonton Macoutes were sinister death squads operating on which island?

10. What is a tog?

11. On which continent is Lake Titicaca?

12. Who lost the Conservative Party leadership contest in 2001?

13. Who was the first British driver to become Formula One World Champion?

14. Which American band's albums include *More Songs About Buildings and Food* and *Little Creatures*?

15. In which county is Bosworth Field where Richard III met his death?

16. What is a takahe?

Answers to page 224
QUIZ 223: **1.** Westland **2.** The Wombles **3.** Winnipeg **4.** French **5.** Steve Heighway and Brian Hall **6.** Lynne Perrie **7.** A flock of starlings landed on the minute hand **8.** Laos **9.** 'Rufus' **10.** Tarrant **11.** Bering Strait **12.** Laa-Laa **13.** Five **14.** German **15.** Alderney **16.** Dachshund

Quiz 222

Answers on page 225

1. Which club are the only founder members of the Football League still in existence never to have won the FA Cup?

2. What is the world's only poisonous bird?

3. Which country has a brand of soft drink called Pshitt?

4. What is the Welsh for Wales?

5. Of which trade union organisation was Lech Walesa the leader?

6. Stromboli was a villain in which Disney film?

7. Which American singer was born Leslie Charles?

8. Who won Best Actor Oscars in both 1993 and 1994?

9. What was invented by the mother of Monkee Michael Nesmith?

10. What links Jim Reeves, Eddie Cochran and Laurel and Hardy?

11. Who was principal conductor of the London Symphony Orchestra 1968–79?

12. What was April Dancer otherwise known as?

13. What is the world's largest rodent?

14. What is a pochard?

15. On which river does Preston stand?

16. Furze is another name for which bush?

Answers to page 225
QUIZ 224: **1.** Rick Wakeman **2.** Seven **3.** The Netherlands **4.** Pam **5.** Jane Leeves (Daphne) **6.** A desert fox **7.** San Francisco **8.** Edmund Ironside **9.** Doctors **10.** Terence **11.** Southend United **12.** 'Sharon' **13.** Natalie Wood **14.** Pelham Grenville **15.** Venezuela **16.** A Vietnamese musical instrument

Quiz 223

Answers on page 222

1. Over which helicopter company's future did Cabinet ministers Michael Heseltine and Leon Brittan resign in 1986?

2. Who were the most successful chart act of 1974?

3. What is the capital of the Canadian province of Manitoba?

4. What is the official language of Togo?

5. Which two university graduates played for Liverpool FC in the 1970s?

6. Which former *Coronation Street* actress appeared on the same bill as both The Beatles and The Rolling Stones in her days as a club singer?

7. What put Big Ben back by five minutes in 1945?

8. The New Kip is the currency in which country?

9. What was the nickname of King William II of England?

10. What was the fictional setting of *Howards' Way*?

11. What is the name of the strait between Alaska and Siberia?

12. Which of the *Teletubbies* is yellow?

13. How many times did Björn Borg win the men's singles title at Wimbledon?

14. What nationality was the inventor of the Bunsen burner?

15. What is the third largest of the Channel Islands?

16. What dog's name means 'badger-hound'?

Answers to page 222
QUIZ 221: **1.** Tennessee Williams **2.** Raquel Welch **3.** Spanish **4.** 1979 **5.** Raith Rovers **6.** The Tourists **7.** The Hitch-Hiker's Guide to the Galaxy **8.** Tonga **9.** Haiti **10.** A unit of measure of thermal insulation **11.** South America **12.** Kenneth Clarke **13.** Mike Hawthorn **14.** Talking Heads **15.** Leicestershire **16.** A flightless bird from New Zealand

Quiz 224

Answers on page 223

1. Which keyboard wizard played synthesiser on David Bowie's 'Space Oddity'?

2. How many players are there in a netball team?

3. Enschede is a town in which country?

4. Who was Bobby Ewing's wife in *Dallas*?

5. Which Frasier star was once a Hill's Angel?

6. What kind of animal is a fennec?

7. Where did The Flowerpot Men suggest going in their 1967 hit?

8. Which English king was murdered while sitting on the toilet?

9. What profession did Harry Hill and Anton Chekhov once share?

10. What was Steve McQueen's first name?

11. Which Football League club plays at Roots Hall?

12. What is Rod Stewart's nickname for Elton John?

13. Which Hollywood actress, who had a morbid fear of water, drowned in 1981?

14. What did the initials 'P.G.' in P.G. Wodehouse stand for?

15. In which country are the Angel Falls?

16. What is a torong?

Answers to page 223
QUIZ 222: **1.** Stoke City **2.** The pitohui **3.** France **4.** Cymru **5.** Solidarity **6.** *Pinocchio* **7.** Billy Ocean **8.** Tom Hanks **9.** Correction fluid **10.** In each case, their biggest hit was achieved posthumously **11.** André Previn **12.** The Girl From UNCLE **13.** Capybara **14.** A type of duck **15.** Ribble **16.** Gorse

Quiz 225

Answers on page 228

1. What musical instrument did Benny Goodman play?

2. Which Football League club are nicknamed the 'Quakers'?

3. In which *Carry On* film did Sid James play The Rumpo Kid?

4. Which singer was found hanging in a Sydney hotel room in 1997?

5. Which King of Norway died after slipping on the soap in his bath and banging his head on one of the taps?

6. From which country does the kiwi fruit originate?

7. Which shipping forecast area covers the coastline from Scarborough to Great Yarmouth?

8. Which planet was first located in 1846?

9. Who lived at 52 Festive Road, London, and made daily visits to a local fancy-dress shop?

10. In which city is Temple Meads railway station?

11. Which type of water lathers easily with soap – soft or hard?

12. Who released the 2002 album *3D*?

13. In which sport do teams compete for the Super Bowl?

14. In which city is *Hollyoaks* set?

15. From which country does the singer Dame Kiri Te Kanawa come?

16. What is the longest river in Scotland?

Answers to page 228
QUIZ 227: **1.** His mask **2.** Galley **3.** Yoko Ono **4.** Stammers **5.** Baccara **6.** Geoffrey Chaucer **7.** Cobalt **8.** Clwyd **9.** Foyle **10.** Wheel-clamping **11.** Keith Duffy **12.** Finnish **13.** Jack London **14.** Habeas corpus **15.** Dustin Hoffman **16.** J. Edgar Hoover

Quiz 226

Answers on page 229

1. In which year was the Wall Street crash?

2. Where do the England rugby union team play home matches?

3. In which county is Melton Mowbray?

4. What method of weaponry was first used at the Battle of the Somme in 1916?

5. Which of the Lipari Islands has an active volcano?

6. Who starred in *Patriot Games* and *The Fugitive*?

7. What is the name of Michael Schumacher's younger brother who is also a Formula One driver?

8. Who was US Vice-President from 1989 to 1993?

9. To what did Isaac Pitman lend his name?

10. Which girl group backed Martha Reeves?

11. In which American state is the industrial city of Pittsburgh?

12. From 1899, who painted a series of water lilies in the garden of his house at Giverny, Normandy?

13. Which brother of Martha was raised by Jesus from the dead?

14. Which English horse race starts in Cambridgeshire and ends in Suffolk?

15. Which Western hero was 'king of the wild frontier'?

16. How many pints are there in a quart?

Answers to page 229
QUIZ 228: **1.** Manic Street Preachers **2.** Princess Anne (to Capt. Mark Phillips) **3.** Norman Scott **4.** Umbrella **5.** Exeter **6.** 'The Terrible' **7.** Machu Picchu **8.** Rumpole of the Bailey **9.** Zither **10.** Leeds **11.** William McGonagall **12.** Molotov cocktail **13.** *Endurance* **14.** Somalia **15.** Eden and Esk **16.** Quasi-Autonomous Non-Governmental Organisation

Quiz 227

Answers on page 226

1. What did the Lone Ranger never remove in public?

2. What is the name for a ship's kitchen?

3. Of whom did Joan Rivers once say: 'If I found her floating in my pool, I'd punish my dog'?

4. What did Bruce Willis, Harvey Keitel and Sir Winston Churchill all have to overcome?

5. Which Spanish duo sang: 'Yes Sir, I Can Boogie'?

6. Who wrote *The Canterbury Tales*?

7. What chemical element has the symbol Co?

8. Colwyn Bay is situated in which county of North Wales?

9. On which river does Londonderry stand?

10. What new experiment brought misery to London motorists in 1983?

11. Which member of Boyzone joined the cast of *Coronation Street* in 2002?

12. What nationality was the composer Sibelius?

13. Who wrote the novels *Call of the Wild* and *White Fang*?

14. Which legal term means 'you may have the body' in Latin?

15. Who won Academy Awards for his performances in *Kramer vs Kramer* and *Rain Man*?

16. Who became director of the FBI in 1924?

Answers to page 226
QUIZ 225: **1.** Clarinet **2.** Darlington **3.** *Carry On Cowboy* **4.** Michael Hutchence **5.** Haakon VII
6. China **7.** Humber **8.** Neptune **9.** Mr Benn **10.** Bristol **11.** Soft **12.** TLC **13.** American Football
14. Chester **15.** New Zealand **16.** Tay

Quiz 228

Answers on page 227

1. James Dean Bradfield is the lead singer with which band?

2. Which member of the royal family was married on 14 November 1973?

3. Who was former Liberal leader Jeremy Thorpe accused of conspiring to murder?

4. In Dickensian London, what was a gamp?

5. St David's railway station serves which West Country city?

6. What was the nickname of Russian ruler Ivan IV?

7. Which lost city of the Incas was rediscovered in the Peruvian Andes by Hiram Bingham in 1911?

8. Which TV character referred to his wife as 'she who must be obeyed'?

9. What musical instrument did Shirley Abicair play?

10. Headingley cricket ground is located in which city?

11. Which 19th-century Scottish poet was renowned for his appalling verse?

12. What kind of cocktail was popular with Resistance groups during the Second World War?

13. What was the name of the ship abandoned by Ernest Shackleton during his 1914–16 Antarctic expedition?

14. Mogadishu is the capital of which African nation?

15. The estuaries of which two rivers form the Solway Firth?

16. For what is quango an acronym?

Answers to page 227
QUIZ 226: **1.** 1929 **2.** Twickenham **3.** Leicestershire **4.** Tank **5.** Stromboli **6.** Harrison Ford **7.** Ralf **8.** Dan Quayle **9.** A form of shorthand **10.** The Vandellas **11.** Pennsylvania **12.** Claude Monet **13.** Lazarus **14.** The Cesarewitch **15.** Davy Crockett **16.** Two

Quiz 229

Answers on page 232

1. After running out of ammunition at the Battle of Lepanto in 1571, with what did the Turks pelt Austrian soldiers?

2. Who were the first British group to top the US singles chart?

3. Which US presidential candidate went on *Rowan and Martin's Laugh-In* to say 'Sock it to me'?

4. Behind Greenland, what is the second largest island in the world?

5. Malaria is caused by which insect?

6. Tresco Airport is on which islands?

7. Which actor's films have included *Ricochet, Crimson Tide* and *Courage Under Fire*?

8. Who was the last British golfer to win the Open?

9. What does the surname of former German Chancellor Helmut Kohl mean in English?

10. Whom did John Hinckley attempt to assassinate in 1981?

11. What type of commercials did ITV ban in 1965?

12. What metric unit of area is equal to 100 acres or 10,000 square metres?

13. Who wrote *Hedda Gabler*?

14. What is a teasel?

15. What links Prince Andrew and Leslie Ash?

16. Which TV crimebuster used to sign off with the words 'Keep 'em peeled'?

Answers to page 232
QUIZ 231: **1.** Warren Beatty **2.** Safety razor **3.** Hoosiers **4.** Fremantle **5.** British Academy of Film and Television Arts **6.** Manama **7.** Bailey bridge **8.** The First Crusade **9.** Crustacean **10.** Javelin **11.** Barry **12.** 1989 **13.** H_2SO_4 **14.** Anthony Eden **15.** Group of 19th-century US writers from New York State **16.** English Civil War

Quiz 230

Answers on page 233

1. In which country is the Vestre Mardola waterfall?

2. The name of which European capital city means 'merchants' harbour'?

3. Of which co-star did Tony Curtis allegedly say: 'It's like kissing Hitler'?

4. Aaron Kosminski, James Maybrick and Dr Francis Tumblety were all suspected of what?

5. Which King of England died after eating a surfeit of lampreys at a banquet in France?

6. Who is the patron saint of laundry workers?

7. Which guitarist is known as 'Old Slow Hand'?

8. Who was the first foreign football manager to win the Premiership?

9. What was the name of the bear in *Rainbow*?

10. Whom did James Callaghan defeat in the 1976 Labour leadership contest?

11. Which show opened in London in 1970, promising 'an evening of elegant erotica'?

12. Which spy escaped from Wormwood Scrubs in 1966?

13. Which town is the administrative headquarters of Dyfed?

14. Which game was invented in 1875 by British army officers serving with the Devonshire Regiment in India?

15. Which resort was the setting for the first Butlin's holiday camp?

16. What is a sirocco?

Answers to page 233
QUIZ 232: **1.** Bruce Willis **2.** Exeter City **3.** 1976 **4.** Kane **5.** Sir Walter Scott **6.** Bartholomew Diaz **7.** *Burke's Peerage* **8.** Hurricane **9.** Seven **10.** Kentucky **11.** Zebra **12.** Rowing **13.** *Doctor Who* **14.** Sri Lanka **15.** Purple **16.** St Lawrence River

Quiz 231

Answers on page 230

1. Which Hollywood star was once employed as a rat catcher by a theatre in Washington DC?

2. What was invented by King Camp Gillette in 1895?

3. What are inhabitants of Indiana known as?

4. Which Australian port is located at the mouth of the Swan River?

5. What does BAFTA stand for?

6. What is the capital of Bahrain?

7. To which Second World War device did Donald Coleman Bailey lend his name?

8. What did Peter the Hermit lead in 1095?

9. Crabs, lobsters and shrimps are all members of which class of creatures?

10. In which field event does Jan Zelezny specialise?

11. Which building worker from *Auf Wiedersehen, Pet* used to be a stalwart of the West Bromwich and District Table Tennis League?

12. In which year was the Berlin Wall dismantled?

13. What is the chemical formula for sulphuric acid?

14. Which British Prime Minister resigned following the Suez crisis?

15. Who were the Knickerbocker School?

16. In which war was the Battle of Marston Moor?

Answers to page 230
QUIZ 229: **1.** Oranges and lemons **2.** The Tornados ('Telstar') **3.** Richard Nixon **4.** New Guinea **5.** Mosquito **6.** Scilly Isles **7.** Denzel Washington **8.** Paul Lawrie **9.** Cabbage **10.** Ronald Reagan **11.** Cigarette commercials **12.** Hectare **13.** Henrik Ibsen **14.** A prickly herb **15.** Both were born on 19 February 1960 **16.** Shaw Taylor (*Police 5*)

Quiz 232

Answers on page 231

1. Of whom did Cybill Shepherd say: 'His idea of a romantic kiss was to go "blaaah" and gag me with his tongue'?

2. Which Football League club are nicknamed 'The Grecians'?

3. In which year did Brotherhood of Man win the Eurovision Song Contest?

4. What is the surname of Handy Andy from *Changing Rooms*?

5. Who wrote *Ivanhoe*?

6. Who was the first European to sail around the Cape of Good Hope?

7. What is the *Genealogical and Heraldic History of the Peerage, Baronetage, and Knightage of the United Kingdom* more commonly known as?

8. What is a 'willy-willy' to Australians?

9. How many events are there in the heptathlon?

10. Which is America's Bluegrass State?

11. What breed of animal did the extinct quagga most resemble?

12. In which sport do participants compete for Doggett's Coat and Badge?

13. Which long-running British TV sci-fi series began in 1963 the day after President Kennedy's assassination?

14. Jaffna, Galle and Negombo are ports in which country?

15. What colour are the flowers of the saffron?

16. Which river does Canada's Victoria Jubilee Bridge cross?

Answers to page 231
QUIZ 230: **1.** Norway **2.** Copenhagen **3.** Marilyn Monroe **4.** *Being Jack the Ripper* **5.** Henry I **6.** St Veronica **7.** Eric Clapton **8.** Arsène Wenger (1998) **9.** Bungle **10.** Michael Foot **11.** *Oh Calcutta!* **12.** George Blake **13.** Carmarthen **14.** Snooker **15.** Skegness **16.** A wind

Quiz 233

Answers on page 236

1. Which US comedy actor was once offered a trial with the Green Bay Packers American Football team?

2. What links Sharon Stone, Nigel Mansell and John Fashanu?

3. What was the Manic Street Preachers' first UK number one?

4. In which year did the state of Israel come into being?

5. Which Beach Boy drowned in a boating accident off California in 1983?

6. What was the name of the *Monty Python* character who had a knotted handkerchief on his head?

7. Who resigned as West German Chancellor in 1974 after an East German spy was discovered working in his office?

8. Which is the most recent county to join the County Cricket Championship?

9. What is a mistral?

10. What colour are the flowers of mimosa?

11. Mahon and Ciudadela are towns on which Mediterranean island?

12. The monstera is better known as which indoor climbing plant?

13. What form of gambling was introduced to Britain in 1922?

14. On which racecourse is the Welsh Grand National run?

15. What was Susan Brown's claim to fame in the world of rowing?

16. What was the Christian name of TV detective Cannon?

Answers to page 236
QUIZ 235: **1.** Henry Cooper **2.** Bruce Jenner **3.** Coleridge **4.** Colchester **5.** Freetown **6.** Superman **7.** The Hollies **8.** Terns **9.** Percussion **10.** Cycling **11.** Cumbria **12.** Tracey in *Birds of a Feather* **13.** Apollo **14.** 2004 **15.** Minnesota **16.** Cheesemaking

Quiz 234

Answers on page 237

1. In 1978, which woman was accused of kidnapping and sexually abusing a Mormon?

2. Whose motto was 'spend, spend, spend'?

3. Which boy band's 1993 album was titled *Walthamstow*?

4. For which country does Jason McAteer play international football?

5. Who was named Best Actress at the 1999 Academy Awards for *Boys Don't Cry*?

6. A convalescent visit by which king gave Bognor its suffix of Regis?

7. Who directed *Casablanca*?

8. On which English moor would you come across Brown Willy?

9. Who was defeated by Ronald Reagan in the 1980 US Presidential election?

10. Which US secretary of state won the Nobel Peace Prize in 1973?

11. Who did Robson Green play in *Soldier, Soldier*?

12. On which river does Mainz stand?

13. Who were the two principal families in *Soap*?

14. Which football team plays at Pittodrie?

15. Who composed the operas *Manon* and *Le Cid*?

16. What is an orfe?

Answers to page 237
QUIZ 236: **1.** Velcro **2.** 'January February' **3.** Poethlyn (1918, 1919) **4.** Waldo **5.** Cherries **6.** St Helena **7.** Seville **8.** Lillehammer **9.** Wild ass **10.** Dorothy Parker **11.** Cher **12.** Lee **13.** Ayr **14.** Gwyneth Paltrow **15.** Harold Robbins **16.** River Lossie

Quiz 235

Answers on page 234

1. Who was the first person to be named BBC Sports Personality of the Year twice?

2. Which 1976 Olympic gold medallist went on to star in *CHiPS*?

3. Whose poems included 'The Ancient Mariner' and 'Kubla Khan'?

4. Camulodunum was the Roman name for which English town?

5. What is the capital of Sierra Leone?

6. Which superhero was created by Jerome Siegel and Joseph Shuster?

7. Which group had hits with 'Sorry Suzanne' and 'I Can't Tell the Bottom From the Top'?

8. What can be common, Arctic or sooty?

9. To what group of musical instruments does the vibraphone belong?

10. At which sport was Englishman Tommy Simpson a champion?

11. In which county is Whitehaven?

12. Which sitcom character had a son called Garthy?

13. Who was the Roman god of the Sun?

14. When is the next Chinese year of the monkey?

15. Which American state is known as the Gopher State?

16. Whey is the watery by-product of which process?

Answers to page 234
QUIZ 233: **1.** Bill Cosby **2.** All are black belts at karate **3.** 'If You Tolerate This Your Children Will Be Next' **4.** 1948 **5.** Dennis Wilson **6.** Mr Gumby **7.** Willy Brandt **8.** Durham **9.** A wind **10.** Yellow **11.** Menorca **12.** Swiss cheese plant **13.** Football pools **14.** Chepstow **15.** She was the first woman cox in the University Boat Race **16.** Frank

Quiz 236

Answers on page 235

1. What was invented by Georges de Mestral after taking his dog for a walk in the woods?

2. Which two months did Barbara Dickson sing about in 1980?

3. Which was the first horse to win the Grand National twice in the 20th century?

4. What was the name of Mr Magoo's nephew?

5. From which fruit is the spirit kirsch made?

6. On which island did Napoleon die?

7. Which Spanish city was the birthplace of the artists Murillo and Velázquez?

8. In which Norwegian town were the 1994 Winter Olympics held?

9. What is an onager?

10. Which Parker was an American writer and wit?

11. Which 52-year-old topped the singles charts in 1998?

12. What is Miss Piggy's surname?

13. On which racecourse is the Scottish Grand National run?

14. About whom was Sharon Stone speaking when she said: 'She lives in rarefied air that's a little thin. It's like she's not getting quite enough oxygen'?

15. What pseudonym was used by novelist Francis Kane?

16. On which river does Elgin stand?

Answers to page 235
QUIZ 234: **1.** Joyce McKinney **2.** Viv Nicholson **3.** East 17 **4.** Republic of Ireland **5.** Hilary Swank **6.** George V **7.** Michael Curtiz **8.** Bodmin Moor **9.** Jimmy Carter **10.** Henry Kissinger **11.** Dave Tucker **12.** Rhine **13.** The Tates and the Campbells **14.** Aberdeen **15.** Jules Massenet **16.** A fish

Quiz 237

Answers on page 240

1. Who lampooned Dickens with the words: 'One must have a heart of stone to read the death of Little Nell without laughing'?

2. In which city is the newspaper *Dagbladet* published?

3. How many points are scored for a field goal in American football?

4. What is South Africa's unit of decimal currency?

5. What was the title of Sherlock Holmes' first adventure?

6. Which London department store first opened its doors to the public in 1909?

7. Who played the Scarlet Pimpernel in the 1998 TV adaptation?

8. Which American state is known as the Garden State?

9. What is the official language of Argentina?

10. Which team are the only non-English winners of the FA Cup?

11. Who was 'French Kissin' in the USA' in 1986?

12. Which magazine introduced Billy the Fish?

13. Which British cathedral has three spires?

14. Which projectile was originally called Morrison's Flyin' Saucer?

15. Which sport is played with a shuttlecock?

16. Which high-kicking girls stepped to fame on *Sunday Night at the London Palladium*?

Answers to page 240
QUIZ 239: **1.** 21 **2.** Richard Gordon **3.** Cindy Bear **4.** 1,500 metres **5.** Switzerland and Italy
6. Marvin Gaye **7.** *Aladdin* **8.** Frank Leboeuf **9.** Zurich **10.** Dorset **11.** Komodo dragon **12.** Pips
13. Czechoslovakia **14.** Patty Hearst **15.** Richard Marx **16.** An Indian cart

Quiz 238

Answers on page 241

1. In an average lifetime, a person will walk the equivalent of how many times around the equator?

2. From which London station would you catch a direct train to Doncaster?

3. Which puppet owl created havoc on *Five O'Clock Club*?

4. What does Goat Island separate?

5. What nationality was Marshal Ney?

6. Whose first UK number one single was 'The Most Beautiful Girl in the World'?

7. Which is the largest planet in the solar system?

8. Which Shakespeare play begins: 'If music be the food of love, play on'?

9. What type of tree is a linden?

10. What is a hinny?

11. In which county was artist John Constable born?

12. Which athletics competition was first held in Helsinki in 1983?

13. Which British-born director was responsible for *Alien*?

14. Which actress of *Straw Dogs* fame appeared in *EastEnders* in 2001?

15. St Agnes and Bryher are islands in which group?

16. Which crime writer created Mike Hammer?

Answers to page 241
QUIZ 240: **1.** *Pride and Prejudice* **2.** Morocco **3.** A belt **4.** Richard and Judy **5.** Jim Carrey
6. Bradford **7.** Solomon **8.** Her Majesty's Stationery Office **9.** Barbra Streisand **10.** A marmoset
11. Ethiopia **12.** Space **13.** Ingemar Johansson **14.** Cowslip **15.** Irish **16.** William Thackeray

Quiz 239

Answers on page 238

1. What is the key number in the card game pontoon?

2. Who wrote the *Doctor* books?

3. Who was Yogi Bear's southern sweetheart?

4. What is the final event in the decathlon?

5. Which two countries are linked by the Simplon Pass?

6. Which Motown artist was shot dead by his father during a row in 1984?

7. Jafar was the villain in which Disney film?

8. In football, which French defender moved from Chelsea to Marseille in July 2001?

9. Which is the largest city in Switzerland?

10. In which county is Weymouth?

11. Which is the biggest lizard in the world?

12. What are missing from a navel orange?

13. Who did Brazil's footballers beat in the 1962 World Cup Final?

14. Which heiress turned bank robber in 1974?

15. Which American singer was 'Right Here Waiting' in 1989?

16. What is an ekka?

Answers to page 238
QUIZ 237: **1.** Oscar Wilde **2.** Oslo **3.** Three **4.** Rand **5.** *A Study in Scarlet* **6.** Selfridges **7.** Richard E. Grant **8.** New Jersey **9.** Spanish **10.** Cardiff City **11.** Debbie Harry **12.** *Viz* **13.** Lichfield **14.** Frisbee **15.** Badminton **16.** The Tiller Girls

Quiz 240

Answers on page 239

1. Which Jane Austen novel revolved around the Bennet sisters?

2. The dirham is the currency of which African country?

3. What is a baldric?

4. Which husband and wife left *This Morning* in 2001?

5. Who starred in the movie *Liar Liar*?

6. Which English city houses the National Museum of Photography, Film and Television?

7. In the Old Testament, who was the third king of Israel?

8. What does HMSO stand for?

9. Who starred in and directed *Yentl*?

10. What is a tamarin?

11. In which country is Lake Tana?

12. In 1996, which band reckoned that the female of the species was more deadly than the male?

13. Which Swedish boxer fought for the World Heavyweight title in the early 1960s?

14. *Primula veris* is the Latin name for which plant?

15. What nationality is Samantha Mumba?

16. Which English novelist had the middle name Makepeace?

Answers to page 239
QUIZ 238: **1.** Five **2.** King's Cross **3.** Ollie Beak **4.** The two halves of the Niagara Falls **5.** French **6.** Prince **7.** Jupiter **8.** *Twelfth Night* **9.** Lime tree **10.** The offspring of a female ass by a stallion **11.** Suffolk **12.** World Championships **13.** Ridley Scott **14.** Susan George **15.** Isles of Scilly **16.** Mickey Spillane

Quiz 241

Answers on page 244

1. What stage name did Thomas Terry Hoar Stevens adopt?

2. How many faces does a tetrahedron have?

3. The Jumna is a tributary of which Indian river?

4. Alex Kingston, Patsy Palmer and Letitia Dean have all appeared in which TV series?

5. Alec Stewart and Mark Butcher played cricket for which English county in 2001?

6. What would Alan Titchmarsh do if confronted with a red-hot poker?

7. Who weren't afraid of the Big Bad Wolf?

8. What is the oldest known vegetable?

9. Which American singer took a 'Walk on the Wild Side' in 1973?

10. Who is St Elmo the patron saint of?

11. What is the only mammal with four knees?

12. The San Andreas fault runs through which American state?

13. What is another name for potassium nitrate?

14. Which ball game occupies the largest playing area?

15. Which city is the administrative capital of South Africa?

16. Who starred opposite Dustin Hoffman in *Kramer vs Kramer*?

Answers to page 244
QUIZ 243: **1.** Dylan Thomas **2.** Helga **3.** Orion **4.** *Platoon* **5.** Eros **6.** Michael Stich **7.** Ethiopia **8.** 42 **9.** The Clash **10.** Y-fronts **11.** Potato **12.** On the fruit counter – it's a variety of apple **13.** Pompeii **14.** Dutch **15.** Maxine Peacock **16.** Billie Jean Moffitt

Quiz 242

Answers on page 245

1. What is the name for the male reproductive organ of a flower?

2. Which band's 1998 album was titled *This is Hardcore*?

3. Whereabouts on a cricket pitch would you find a chain?

4. What letter is at the bottom right end of a standard keyboard?

5. Cannock Chase is in which English county?

6. Who appeared as King Arthur in the film *Camelot* with a piece of Elastoplast visible on his neck?

7. Which Cornish detective was created by W.J. Burley?

8. When was the only time all four home international football countries qualified for the World Cup finals?

9. Which American novelist wrote *Of Mice and Men*?

10. What is the Taoiseach?

11. What colour are the flowers of wild garlic?

12. The Aleutian Islands are part of which American state?

13. Which Formula One team are based at Maranello?

14. What was the name of the romantic car salesman on *The Fast Show*?

15. In which century did the Thirty Years' War take place in Europe?

16. Which plant is sometimes known as thrift?

Answers to page 245
QUIZ 244: **1.** Robin Williams **2.** *Friends* **3.** Theodore Roosevelt **4.** Copenhagen **5.** Once **6.** An onion **7.** Hawaii **8.** Octopus **9.** Ayrshire **10.** Leslie Charteris **11.** An Indian tree **12.** Dick Emery **13.** Manila **14.** New Deal **15.** Cod **16.** Guy Ritchie

Quiz 243

Answers on page 242

1. Who wrote *Under Milk Wood*?

2. Who was Herr Flick's right-hand woman in *'Allo 'Allo*?

3. What constellation depicts a hunter with club and shield?

4. Which Oliver Stone movie won an Oscar for Best Picture in 1986?

5. Who was the Greek god of love?

6. Which German won the men's singles at Wimbledon in 1991?

7. In which country is Dallol, the hottest place in the world?

8. How many dots are there on a pair of dice?

9. Which band asked: 'Should I Stay Or Should I Go'?

10. Inspired by a photo of a pair of swimming trunks on the French Riviera, what did underwear manufacturers Coopers introduce to the market in 1934?

11. Which vegetable was used as a windscreen wiper in the early days of motoring?

12. Where might you find a Beauty of Bath at the supermarket?

13. Which town was destroyed by Vesuvius in AD 79?

14. What nationality was the painter Vermeer?

15. Which *Coronation Street* hairdresser was killed by Richard Hillman in 2003?

16. Under what name did Billie Jean King first compete at Wimbledon?

Answers to page 242

QUIZ 241: **1.** Terry-Thomas **2.** Four **3.** Ganges **4.** *Grange Hill* **5.** Surrey **6.** Grow it (it's a perennial plant) **7.** The Three Little Pigs **8.** The pea **9.** Lou Reed **10.** Sailors **11.** Elephant **12.** California **13.** Saltpetre **14.** Polo **15.** Pretoria **16.** Meryl Streep

Quiz 244

Answers on page 243

1. Who played the title role in the film *Popeye*?

2. George Clooney, the Duchess of York and June Whitfield have all guested on which sitcom?

3. Who was the first teddy bear named after?

4. Which European city did Danny Kaye think was 'wonderful, wonderful'?

5. How many times a year does a penguin mate?

6. The ancient Egyptians believed that mixing half of what with beer foam would ward off death?

7. Which American state supplies over a third of the world's commercial pineapples?

8. Which sea creature sometimes eats itself if it becomes unduly stressed?

9. In which Scottish county is Troon golf course?

10. Who created *The Saint*?

11. What is a chaulmoogra?

12. Which comedian's characters included Lampwick, College and Hetty?

13. What is the capital of the Philippines?

14. Which programme did President Franklin Roosevelt introduce in 1933 to counter the Depression?

15. A pollack is a member of which family of fish?

16. Which British film director married Madonna?

Answers to page 243
QUIZ 242: **1.** Stamen **2.** Pulp **3.** Between the wickets (a chain equals 22 yards) **4.** M
5. Staffordshire **6.** Richard Harris **7.** Wycliffe **8.** 1958 **9.** John Steinbeck **10.** The Gaelic name for the Prime Minister of the Irish Republic **11.** White **12.** Alaska **13.** Ferrari **14.** Swiss Toni **15.** 17th
16. Sea pink

Quiz 245

Answers on page 248

1. Which international singing star failed the audition for *Opportunity Knocks*?

2. Which sporting contest is named after an English seed merchant?

3. What is the name of Jim Royle's wife in *The Royle Family*?

4. What animals did Dian Fossey study in Rwanda from 1975?

5. In which county are the Quantock Hills?

6. Which British jockey won the Epsom Derby six times between 1915 and 1925?

7. Forget-me-nots belong to which genus?

8. In which year did the Russian Revolution take place?

9. What nationality was the poet Robert Frost?

10. Which young singer confessed in 1972 that he had no idea where Liverpool was?

11. Which country consumes more Coca-Cola per head than any other?

12. What was Chad capital Ndjamena formerly known as?

13. Which two South American countries fought the Chaco War in the 1930s?

14. Brass is an alloy of which two metals?

15. Which is the smallest state in the USA?

16. 'Charisma', 'Bayleaf' and 'Vaseline' were all characters in which TV series?

Answers to page 248
QUIZ 247: **1.** The Supremes **2.** Miss Piggy **3.** Eurydice **4.** Kookaburra **5.** Green, white and red
6. Laurie Lee **7.** Leicestershire **8.** Carole Lombard **9.** Rigsby (*Rising Damp*) **10.** 39 **11.** Vatican City
12. Kampala **13.** Sixpence **14.** Mrs Bridges **15.** London Bridge **16.** 20

Quiz 246

Answers on page 249

1. In 1990, which then Football League club were banned from wearing shirts advertising Black Death vodka on the grounds of bad taste?

2. What was the name of the dog in *The Herbs*?

3. Who penned *Elegy Written in a Country Churchyard*?

4. Which English king was known as the 'Sailor King'?

5. In which Northern Ireland county is the town of Enniskillen?

6. Who broke Jackie Stewart's record of 27 Formula One Grand Prix wins?

7. Who starred in *On the Waterfront* and *In the Heat of the Night*?

8. Where did Fiddler's Dram go for a day trip in 1979?

9. Which American President was cruelly nicknamed 'The Illinois Baboon' on account of his appearance?

10. Which golfer missed a three-foot putt to win the 1970 British Open and then lost the play-off to fellow countryman Jack Nicklaus?

11. In which US state is the port of Charleston?

12. What is the chemical symbol for potassium?

13. Which baseball player was nicknamed 'The Georgia Peach'?

14. What was the Christian name of the German motor manufacturer Daimler?

15. What is the southernmost point of the English mainland?

16. In which century was the okapi first discovered?

Answers to page 249
QUIZ 248: **1.** The Millennium Bridge **2.** Isobars **3.** Cambridgeshire **4.** Todd Woodbridge and Mark Woodforde **5.** John Huston **6.** Vera Palmer **7.** Praying mantis **8.** Acer **9.** Second World War **10.** Buenos Aires **11.** The Compact Pussycat **12.** Lon Chaney Snr **13.** Don McLean **14.** Nine **15.** Belize **16.** 1990

Quiz 247

Answers on page 246

1. Who were the first female group to top the UK singles charts?

2. With whom did Rudolf Nureyev dance a *pas de deux* on *The Muppet Show*?

3. In Greek mythology, who was the wife of Orpheus?

4. Which bird is also known as the laughing jackass?

5. What colours are the three horizontal stripes on the national flag of Kuwait?

6. Who wrote *Cider with Rosie*?

7. Which county cricket club's Norwich Union League team are known as the Foxes?

8. Which American comedy actress changed her name from Jane Alice Peters?

9. Which TV sitcom character owned a cat called Vienna?

10. How many books are there in the Old Testament?

11. Which is the smallest state in the world?

12. What is the capital of Uganda?

13. Which unit of currency was finally phased out in 1980?

14. What was the name of the cook in *Upstairs, Downstairs*?

15. Which landmark was dismantled and taken to Arizona in 1968?

16. For how many years did Rip Van Winkle sleep?

Answers to page 246

QUIZ 245: **1.** Engelbert Humperdinck **2.** Ryder Cup **3.** Barbara **4.** Gorillas **5.** Somerset **6.** Steve Donoghue **7.** Myosotis **8.** 1917 **9.** American **10.** Little Jimmy Osmond **11.** Iceland **12.** Fort Lamy **13.** Bolivia and Paraguay **14.** Copper and zinc **15.** District of Columbia **16.** *London's Burning*

Quiz 248

Answers on page 247

1. Which walkway opened and closed within two days in the summer of 2000?

2. What is the name of the lines drawn on weather maps linking places with the same atmospheric pressure?

3. In which county is the Isle of Ely?

4. Which tennis pairing were known as the 'Woodies'?

5. Who directed *The Maltese Falcon* and *The African Queen*?

6. What was Jayne Mansfield's real name?

7. The female of which insect frequently bites off the head of the male during reproduction?

8. To which genus does the maple tree belong?

9. The Battle of Anzio took place during which war?

10. Which capital city's name means 'good winds'?

11. What vehicle did Penelope Pitstop drive in *Wacky Races*?

12. Which actor was known as 'The Man of a Thousand Faces'?

13. Who was the subject of Roberta Flack's 'Killing Me Softly With His Song'?

14. How many innings are there in a game of baseball?

15. Which country used to be known as British Honduras?

16. In which year did Adamski have a UK number one with 'Killer'?

Answers to page 247
QUIZ 246: **1.** Scarborough **2.** Dill **3.** Thomas Gray **4.** William IV **5.** Fermanagh **6.** Alain Prost **7.** Rod Steiger **8.** Bangor **9.** Abraham Lincoln **10.** Doug Sanders **11.** South Carolina **12.** K **13.** Ty Cobb **14.** Gottlieb **15.** The Lizard **16.** 20th

Quiz 249

Answers on page 252

1. Which planet has a pink sky?

2. According to old British legend, with which knight did Queen Guinevere have an affair?

3. Which sport – played only in the USA – boasts a World Series?

4. In which mountain country do yak live?

5. Who was *Callan*'s smelly sidekick?

6. Which Righteous Brothers song was used in the 1990 film *Ghost*?

7. Which fashion designer co-owned a shop with Malcolm McLaren?

8. Which envoy to the Archbishop of Canterbury was kidnapped in Beirut in 1987?

9. What colour are the stripes on the flag of Uruguay?

10. What unwanted distinction did Manchester United's Kevin Moran achieve in the 1985 FA Cup Final?

11. Stewart Copeland was the drummer with which successful trio?

12. Who was the unseen doorman in the US sitcom *Rhoda*?

13. Which capital city's pride is a form of saxifrage?

14. The Battle of St Albans was the first round in which conflict?

15. What is a cricket umpire signalling when he raises both arms aloft?

16. What is a jarrah?

Answers to page 252
QUIZ 251: **1.** Les Dawson **2.** Leader of the army **3.** Erasure **4.** Batley **5.** Rimsky-Korsakov **6.** Japan **7.** Scout **8.** 9th **9.** Plover **10.** Backstroke **11.** Leonardo DiCaprio **12.** Lord Reith **13.** Lt Uhura **14.** Penguin **15.** USSR **16.** Centigrade

Quiz 250

Answers on page 253

1. Which bird features on the coat of arms of the state of Louisiana?

2. What colour is the circle on the Japanese national flag?

3. Which adjoining country forms Moldova's western border?

4. Who dedicated his 1998 hit 'Just The Two of Us' to his son Tre?

5. Which king's appendix caused his coronation to be delayed for six weeks?

6. Who joined the cast of *EastEnders* as Alfie Moon in 2002?

7. What nationality was jockey Scobie Breasley?

8. Who was Queen of the Netherlands from 1948 to 1980?

9. Which singer's biggest hit, 'Me and Bobby McGee', was not released until after her death?

10. Which Gertrude was a noted English landscape gardener?

11. Which novelist died from typhoid two months after drinking a glass of tap water in a Paris hotel to prove that it was safe?

12. Which insect can live for over a week with its head cut off?

13. Which writer disappeared following *The Murder of Roger Ackroyd*?

14. Which Football League team had to apologise to their local rivals in September 2001 after calling them 'Scum' on an electronic scoreboard?

15. What is 'indie' short for in music?

16. In which county is Stow-on-the-Wold?

Answers to page 253
QUIZ 252: **1.** 'Buffalo Bill' **2.** 1950 **3.** East Sussex **4.** Small circular dishes **5.** Electrocardiogram **6.** Beth **7.** President de Gaulle **8.** West Indies **9.** Denis Howell **10.** Marlon Brando (*The Godfather*) **11.** Burgos **12.** Nose **13.** Fiji **14.** A ballet movement **15.** France **16.** The Ram Jam Band

Quiz 251

Answers on page 250

1. Who preceded Lily Savage as host of *Blankety Blank*?

2. What does the Japanese word 'shogun' mean?

3. Who took their 'Abba-Esque' EP to number one in 1992?

4. Who were the first winners of the Rugby League Challenge Cup?

5. Who composed the opera *The Snow Maiden*?

6. In which country was actress Liv Ullmann born?

7. What was the name of Tonto's horse?

8. In which century did reindeer become extinct in the wild in the UK?

9. To which family of birds does the lapwing belong?

10. Which is the only swimming stroke not started by a dive?

11. Who starred opposite Claire Danes in the 1996 movie *Romeo & Juliet*?

12. Who was the first managing director of the BBC?

13. Who was head of communications on the starship *Enterprise*?

14. Which is the only bird that walks upright?

15. Who did West Germany beat in the semi-finals of the 1966 World Cup?

16. What is the Celsius temperature scale otherwise known as?

Answers to page 250
QUIZ 249: **1.** Mars **2.** Sir Lancelot **3.** Baseball **4.** Tibet **5.** Lonely **6.** 'Unchained Melody' **7.** Vivienne Westwood **8.** Terry Waite **9.** Blue and white **10.** He was the first player to be sent off in an FA Cup Final **11.** The Police **12.** Carlton **13.** London (London pride) **14.** The Wars of the Roses **15.** A six **16.** A type of eucalyptus tree from Australia

Quiz 252

Answers on page 251

1. What was William Frederick Cody's alter ego?

2. In which year was the Princess Royal born?

3. In which county might you come face to face with the Long Man of Wilmington?

4. What are ramekins?

5. What is ECG an abbreviation for?

6. What was Dr Glover's first name in *Peak Practice*?

7. *The Day of the Jackal* was a novel about the attempted assassination of which world leader?

8. Who won cricket's first World Cup?

9. Whose appointment as minister for drought in 1976 coincided with the sudden end to the summer-long heatwave?

10. Who refused to accept his Best Actor Oscar for 1972 in protest over the plight of American Indians?

11. In which city's cathedral is El Cid buried?

12. What did Cyrano de Bergerac have that was longer than most men's?

13. Viti Levu is the largest of which group of islands?

14. What is a fouetté?

15. Which nation's post-war constitution was known as the Fourth Republic?

16. Which band backed Geno Washington?

Answers to page 251
QUIZ 250: **1.** Pelican **2.** Red **3.** Romania **4.** Will Smith **5.** Edward VII **6.** Shane Richie **7.** Australian **8.** Juliana **9.** Janis Joplin **10.** Gertrude Jekyll **11.** Arnold Bennett **12.** Cockroach **13.** Agatha Christie **14.** Norwich City (apologised to Ipswich Town) **15.** Independent **16.** Gloucestershire